COUNTERPOINT
BASED ON
EIGHTEENTH CENTURY PRACTICE

I - vii° - IV - V - I
over pedal point

COUNTERPOINT

BASED ON

EIGHTEENTH CENTURY PRACTICE

KENT KENNAN

PROFESSOR OF MUSIC

THE UNIVERSITY OF TEXAS

Author of
The Technique of Orchestration

ENGLEWOOD CLIFFS, N.J.

PRENTICE-HALL, INC.

LIBRARY OF CONGRESS
CATALOG CARD NO.: 59–7075

First printing .... February , 1959
Second printing .... March , 1960
Third printing ...... November , 1961
Fourth printing ...... February , 1963

PRINTED IN THE UNITED STATES OF AMERICA

18362-C

Contents

Contents

Contents

Preface

Counterpoint texts have tended to fall into two categories: those that cover the elementary stages but seldom go beyond the writing of inventions, if that far; and those that include no elementary work but concentrate on invertible counterpoint, canon and fugue. Obviously, neither type is satisfactory as a complete text for a course that must start at the beginning and progress through a study of fugue. This book represents an attempt to provide a text comprehensive enough for such a course, in a form that can be covered during a year. Ideally, of course, a longer time should be allowed for a study of this scope; however, in many schools the schedule allows no more than a year. Given such a time restriction, how should the subject be approached, and what is the minimum amount of material to be included?

First, it seems axiomatic that the student should learn some of the basic techniques of contrapuntal writing. In this book a modified species approach has been employed—"species" in that exercises using the basic rhythmic ratios are to be done at the start—"modified" in the sense that the whole-note *cantus firmus* is abandoned in favor of melodies that come closer to being real music and have a sense of harmonic rhythm. Also, some of the more rigid restrictions of "Fux-style" counterpoint are waived. Florid (fifth) species is not undertaken as such, inasmuch as it resembles closely the free counterpoint which students will write in later projects.

Second, the student should become acquainted with the outstanding contrapuntal techniques that are associated with eighteenth-century counterpoint—that is, invention, canon, chorale forms, invertible counterpoint, and fugue. This should be done not only through analysis but through the writing of examples. Except, perhaps, for work done by students majoring in composition and theory, these writing projects are not likely to be polished or highly original efforts. Nevertheless, they have a real value in providing a working knowledge of contrapuntal forms.

The author is aware that in attempting to compress what he has outlined here into a book of this size he runs the risk of over-condensation. Yet he hopes that readers will gain at least the essentials of the forms and devices discussed; an attempt has been made to concentrate on those essentials and to avoid becoming bogged down in minor details and exceptions.

Much as a knowledge of the C clefs is to be admired and encouraged, experience has shown that the average student does not have a real working command of them, and they have consequently not been used in this book. If individual students who have already acquired some facility in them choose to use them in their work, well and good. But it seems doubtful that the problem of learning them should be coupled with the problem of learning counterpoint.

The choice of the eighteenth-century style as the basis for this text does not imply any lack of regard for the beauties of sixteenth-century counterpoint or any suggestion that one style is more worth while than the other as an object of study. An intimate acquaintance with both is part of the background of every well-trained musician. The author does feel, however, that the eighteenth-century style is best taught first (even though it did not come first) simply because it underlies the great body of music that is most familiar to students.

In many counterpoint texts one finds a curious and irritating tone, aptly described by Grove's Dictionary as "a tendency to surround the art with an air of mystery and to make initiation into it something of an ordeal, fraught with difficulties, with dry-as-dust rules and prohibitions." A particular effort has been made to avoid that tone here. Although there will necessarily be some directions and "prohibitions," they will be based as much as possible on the actual practice of composers in a given period rather than on a mysterious and abstract set of rules whose source of authority is vague and questionable.

The material in this book and in the COUNTERPOINT WORKBOOK has been tested through use in the classes in eighteenth-century counterpoint at the University of Texas.

The author's sincere thanks go to Dr. Paul Pisk, Mrs. Janet McGaughey and Dr. Richard Hoppin for their careful examination of the manuscript and their many helpful suggestions; also to Miss Jean Cassel for her unfailing kindness in connection with library materials.

KENT KENNAN

Suggestions for the Use of This Book

At the end of each chapter a list of suggested assignments is given. The specific musical exercises referred to in some of those assignments are contained in a COUNTERPOINT WORKBOOK (Prentice-Hall, Inc.). It is not intended that all the assignments be covered by any one student or class; projects of varying difficulty and scope have been included with a view to meeting the requirements of different teaching situations.

The material in this book need not be presented in the exact order used here. For example, students usually find canons easier to write than inventions; consequently some teachers may wish to jump from Chapter V (Exercises in Two-Voice Counterpoint) to Chapter IX on canons, and to do some writing of two-voice canons before going on with inventions and three-voice counterpoint. Another possible plan is to skip Chapters VI and VIII on inventions until all the other chapters through IX have been covered. Still another variation involves taking the chapters in the order given but limiting the work on inventions to reading and analysis for the time being, the actual writing of inventions being put off until later.

In any case, the author believes that there is a decided advantage in interspersing the writing assignments with those calling only for analysis, in order to give variety and some relief from an overly continuous diet of written work.

As an illustration of a practical application of counterpoint study, one or more projects in the writing of descants for hymns could be included. These can probably be done most effectively in class; the hymn is put on the blackboard, the principles of descant-writing are discussed, and students then contribute phrases for the descant; finally the hymn and descant are sung by the class. A similar project involves writing a counter-melody for a march which has been given in condensed-score form.

It is strongly recommended that students be given the opportunity to *hear* in class as many examples as possible of the forms they are studying. While pianists and organists ordinarily have considerable acquaintance with the Bach Inventions and *The Well Tempered Clavier*, other students often do not.

Suggestions

And it is obviously unreasonable to expect a student to imitate a technique which is not familiar to him through listening. Furthermore, performance of music by members of the class (or, barring that, via records) can do much to stimulate interest and promote a feeling of counterpoint as a live—and lively—art.

KENT KENNAN

¶ Introduction

1

Ever since music has utilized independent lines or voices, composers and theorists have concerned themselves with the principles involved in setting one voice against another effectively. Probably the best known of all treatises on counterpoint is Fux's *Gradus ad Parnassum,* published in 1725. About it Ernest Newman says, "Directly or indirectly it is the foundation of practically all the methods of teaching counterpoint during the last two hundred years." Written originally in Latin and since translated into many languages, the book is in the form of a dialogue between the teacher, Aloysius (intended by Fux to represent Palestrina), and Josephus, the pupil who wishes to learn composition. We know that Mozart worked the exercises in the *Gradus* while he was still a boy; that both Haydn and Albrechtsberger absorbed its contents, as did their counterpoint pupil, Beethoven; and that most of the outstanding composers of the nineteenth century studied counterpoint according to Fux's principles, as passed on by Albrechtsberger and Cherubini.

Unfortunately these writers and others of their day were either unaware of the tremendous contribution made by J. S. Bach or chose to ignore it because Bach's practices were at variance with what they taught. Thus there existed a curious situation in which a system of counterpoint purporting to be the authoritative approach to the subject persisted even though it failed to take into account the greatest contrapuntal music of a full century earlier.

This, then, is a bit of the historical background of "strict counterpoint." There has long been disagreement as to exactly what that term means. In general, it refers to a technique that is closest to sixteenth-century practice, the style being essentially vocal. Some teachers have retained the modal approach, à la Fux, while others have discarded it in favor of our "major-

1

minor" system.   For all its value as a discipline, strict counterpoint has sometimes stressed a kind of hypothetical style based more on pedagogically devised restrictions than on the practice of the sixteenth century or any other period.   Approached in this fashion, it tends to produce "music that never was on sea or land," as R. O. Morris puts it in his *Contrapuntal Technique of the Sixteenth Century.*

A term parallel to "strict counterpoint" is "free counterpoint," which generally implies the use of eighteenth-century instrumental models.

The tendency today is to abandon the somewhat ambiguous terms "strict" and "free" and to teach counterpoint on the basis of what was practiced in the sixteenth and eighteenth centuries.   Because the styles of these two periods differ in spirit, technical construction, and usually the use of a text, they call for different approaches—that is, different courses, or at least separate parts of the same course.   An attempt to fuse them into one composite style will only result in a synthetic model which has no counterpart in actual music.

The present volume deals entirely with eighteenth-century ("baroque" or "Bach-style") counterpoint, and chiefly with instrumental music.   But it is important to understand at the outset that the basic principles of eighteenth-century counterpoint actually apply in a broad sense to contrapuntal music clear through Wagner's day—and even in much music of the twentieth century.   That is, in spite of the many changes and stylistic innovations in music during the past three hundred years, the fundamental approach to polyphony remained more or less constant until the late nineteenth century. At that time, impressionism and other trends brought about certain changes in viewpoint, and there has since been a healthy revival of interest in sixteenth-century methods on the part of composers.   The point being made here is that the term "Bach-style counterpoint" is far more inclusive than the literal meaning of the phrase might suggest.   In studying that type of counterpoint we are not limiting our interest to the music of Bach or even to the music of the eighteenth century; rather, we are concentrating on models from that period because they afford the clearest examples of a contrapuntal technique that underlies much of the music of three centuries.

In the process of explaining the meaning of the term counterpoint to his student Josephus, Fux's Aloysius says, "It is necessary for you to know that in earlier times, instead of our modern notes, dots or points were used.   Thus, one used to call a composition in which point was set against or counter to point, *counterpoint.*"   As a technique this might be defined as the art of combining two or more melodic lines in a musically satisfying way.   Included in this definition is the assumption that each line is good in itself; and the

2

phrase "a musically satisfying way" implies among other things that the lines will be independent yet coordinate in feeling.

While counterpoint puts primary emphasis on the linear or horizontal aspect of music, it also concerns the vertical combinations of tones; that is, the lines heard in combination must outline clear-cut and strong harmonic progressions. As Oldroyd puts it in his book, *The Technique and Spirit of Fugue*, "Counterpoint is the flight of melodic tracery between one harmony and another." R. O. Morris, in his *Foundations of Practical Harmony and Counterpoint*, sums up the vertical-horizontal relationship neatly: "Harmony and counterpoint are not two different things but merely two different ways of regarding the same thing."

In closing, two of Aloysius' admonitions to Josephus might be offered. The first concerns the necessity of persistence in order to become proficient at counterpoint:

> Always remember:
> drops wear down the stone
> not by strength but by constant falling.

The second expresses a prediction which every writer of a textbook fondly hopes he will help to make a reality:

If you will work thus you will be delighted to see the way in which light gradually illuminates what had been obscure and how in some manner the curtain of darkness seems to be drawn away.

¶ The Single
Melodic Line

2

MELODIC CURVE

The first requisite of a good melodic line is a sense of direction, of clear-cut melodic "curve." The possibilities for the shape of the curve are too numerous to catalog completely, but certain general patterns can be cited. There is, for example, the type that begins at its lowest pitch and moves basically upward to its highest point:

EX. 1   BEETHOVEN - Sonata, Op. 14, No. 1 (Piano)
Allegro

And the opposite of this is illustrated in the following:

EX. 2   BACH - French Suite No. 5 (Gavotte)

In both these melodies there are reversals of direction and secondary curves within the broad over-all curve. These, however, do not alter the basic directional feeling that each melody conveys as a whole.

4

A more frequently found curve is that in which the line moves from a low point to a high point and then subsides to a lower pitch. The high point may occur anywhere in the course of the melody, but is perhaps most often seen in the last half. Example 3 illustrates this melodic shape.

EX. 3   BACH - W. T. C., * Vol. II, Fugue 11

The opposite pattern—one which starts high, dips down, and then ascends— is shown next.

EX. 4   BEETHOVEN - Sonata, Op. 28 (Piano)

Some melodies involve a kind of pivotal pattern, in which the line centers around a particular note or area:

EX. 5   FRANCK - Symphony in D minor

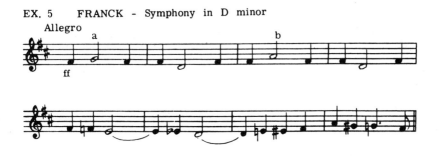

* This abbreviation is used in examples throughout this book to refer to Bach's *The Well Tempered Clavier.*

5

Notice, though, that in such cases the *intentional* nature of the return to the pivotal note is obvious to the ear. Note also that the use of this type of pattern may still involve a sense of progression and direction—for instance, in Example 5, from the note at *a* to the note at *b*. Unless a clearly intentional pattern is present, as it is in this last example, a melody that keeps doubling back over the same notes is almost certain to sound repetitious and lacking in a sense of direction.

Whatever curve is involved, it is generally best to avoid having a line ascend to the same *high* point more than once, as that is likely to cancel out a feeling of pitch climax. On the other hand, a sense of climax in melodic lines is not dependent on pitch alone. Other factors such as duration (agogic accent), dynamic values, and placement of notes within the melody enter in. For example, a note which, in terms of pitch, would not command particular attention may be made more important by means of a longer value or dynamic accent, while a relatively high pitch which is passed over quickly may not have the climactic effect it would have if sustained.

RANGE

Melodies vary widely as to range; some are confined within the interval of a 5th or 6th, whereas others have a compass of two octaves or more. Probably the average range in invention motives and fugue subjects of the period we are considering is about an octave. Example 6 shows melodies with narrow and wide ranges, respectively.

EX. 6   BACH - W. T. C., Vol. I, Fugue 8

BEETHOVEN - Sonata, Op. 10, No. 3 (Piano)

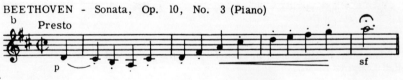

UNDERLYING STRUCTURE

In many melodies a skeletal structure—a kind of line within a line—is apparent to the ear, the other notes having a decorative, somewhat less important role.   Example 7 shows the reduction of a rather ornate melody to its skeletal form.

EX. 7   HANDEL - The Messiah

HARMONIC IMPLICATIONS

Some melodies, such as the one in Example 8, outline a definite harmonic background.

EX. 8   BACH - Two-Part Invention No. 4

On the other hand, a line such as the following conveys very little harmonic suggestion in itself, and is highly dependent for interest on the harmony that is actually heard with it.

EX. 9   BEETHOVEN - Symphony No. 7

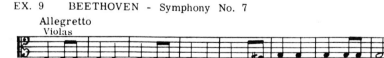

7

For obvious reasons, the first of these two types (Example 8) is by far the more frequent and successful in contrapuntal music.

Certain melodies achieve a sense of harmonic definition by presenting, in effect, two lines heard alternately (Example 10).

If the two lines implied in this passage were written as such, they would look approximately like this:

The compound type of line shown in Example 10 occurs frequently in Bach's music, particularly in his works for unaccompanied violin, where a sense of harmonic completeness might be difficult to achieve otherwise.

The term "harmonic rhythm" is often used to describe the pattern of harmonic change in music. Although a harmonic basis is likely to be most definite when two or more melodies are involved, harmonic rhythm is apparent even in a single melodic line that suggests a specific chordal background.

In Example 8, for instance, the harmonic rhythm is 𝅗𝅥. | 𝅗𝅥. | 𝅗𝅥. | 𝅗𝅥. (one chord per measure). Another frequent arrangement, in measures of two or four beats, is that of a harmonic change on every other beat. And in much music —chorales, for example—as well as in most of the "species" exercises to be done in connection with this book, a chord change on each beat is the usual pattern. Harmonic rhythms in which a harmony lasts more than a measure are fairly common; those involving harmonic durations of less than a beat are also possible, though less frequent. Of course the pattern need not remain constant, and the mixed use of various harmonic rhythms allows for many different composite patterns. More will be said on this subject in a later chapter.

8

Notice that in the style being considered the tonality is usually established at or near the beginning of a melody by inclusion of the tonic note, and by suggestions of tonic harmony. The melodies quoted so far illustrate this point. Notice, too, that tonic harmony occurring at the *end* of a phrase or section normally falls on a "strong" beat (the first or third in a measure of four beats, the first in a measure of two or three beats).

OTHER CONSIDERATIONS

So far we have done no more than to touch briefly on some of the many possibilities in melodic curve and on some factors in melodic construction. We should now consider certain specific points involved in successful melody writing:

1) The natural tendencies of the fourth, sixth, and seventh scale steps, the so-called "active" steps, must be respected. The second scale step is sometimes considered active as well, but it has less sense of gravitational pull, so to speak. Its basic tendency is down to the tonic note, but it often moves up to the third of the scale instead. Example 12 shows the tendencies of the active tones in C major.

EX. 12

But if approached as shown in Example 13*a,* these same tones move more naturally in the opposite direction. Sometimes they leap to another active tone, in which case the tendency of the first note is waived and the manner of resolution derives from the tendency of the second note (Example 13*b*).

EX. 13

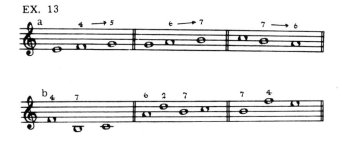

9

In minor, the same tendencies apply. The *melodic* minor scale (Example 14) is the one normally used in this style.

EX. 14

As a very general rule, ascending passages employ the ascending form of the melodic minor, descending passages the descending form. But harmonic background also plays an important part in the choice of one or the other of these scale forms. There are times when the ascending form must be used in a descending passage in order to imply the (major) dominant chord (Example 15*a*). Sometimes the descending form is seen in an ascending passage when the (minor) subdominant is to be implied (Example 15*b*).

EX. 15   BACH - W. T. C., Vol. I, Fugue 2

BACH - W. T. C., Vol. I, Fugue 4

In any case, the awkward and unvocal interval of an augmented 2nd that occurs between the unaltered sixth scale step and the raised seventh step (A-flat to B-natural in C minor) is generally avoided in melodic lines. Virtually the only case in which it may be used successfully in a melodic way is in a passage that outlines a diminished seventh chord (Example 16).

10

The Single Melodic Line

EX. 16   BRAHMS - Symphony No. 1

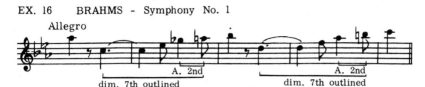

On the other hand, the melodic interval of a diminished 7th between the unaltered sixth scale step and the raised seventh step of the octave *below* is entirely acceptable, and is found frequently in music of the baroque and classical periods (see Examples 3 and 4 in Chapter 14, pages 189 and 191).

2) Even in a single melodic line certain tones may be heard as nonharmonic to implied harmonies and should be resolved.   Since this point is much more likely to arise as a problem in connection with two-voice exercises to be done later, further discussion of it is being reserved for Chapter 4.

3) When two or more leaps are made in the same direction, the ear interprets all the notes as belonging to the same harmony, assuming that none of them is clearly nonharmonic.   Therefore, consecutive leaps should involve only notes which form a harmony acceptable in the style being used.   In the idiom we are studying, such successions as the following are ruled out for this reason:

EX. 17

If, however, the last note in each case is heard as being nonharmonic and is then resolved, all of the successions become usable.   For instance, the B-flat at the beginning of the second measure in Example 18 is nonharmonic to the F major harmony.

EX. 18   BRAHMS - Violin Concerto

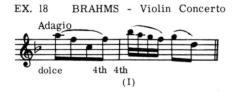

Reversing the direction of the second interval in each succession in Example 17 would make them all acceptable, since the sense of implied harmony would then be cancelled out.

4) Even when they fit into the same implied harmony, two *large* leaps (say of a 6th or more) in the same direction should be avoided, since they would tend to take the line too far in one direction too suddenly, and would bring about a lack of melodic balance (Example 19*a*). After a large leap it is usually best to have the melody turn in the opposite direction (Example 19*b*).

EX. 19

5) As a very general rule, a leap followed by stepwise motion is preferable to stepwise motion followed by a leap (Example 20). *when moving in same direction*

EX. 20

The faster the movement of the notes involved, and the wider the leap, the more objectionable is this step-leap succession. Consequently, it is most likely to become a problem when the leap is between the last fraction of one beat and the next beat. In slower-moving note values the result is slightly better, though still weak (Example 21*a*). The placement of the leap in relation to the harmonic rhythm is also a factor; if the leap is from a strong beat to a weak beat, the result is more likely to be acceptable (Examples 21*b* and *c*).

EX. 21

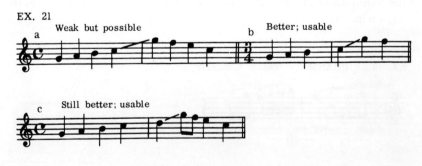

6) There should be some corroboration of musical elements, melodic or rhythmic or both. Melodic corroboration may be achieved by the actual repetition of an element—anything from a small figure to an entire phrase or section. The repetition may occur successively, as in Example 22, or after intervening material.

EX. 22   MOZART - Piano Concerto No. 26, D major (K. 537)

Sequence, in which a melodic element recurs on another scale step, is much more frequent than literal repetition in this style, and is an extremely common and important device in contrapuntal music of the eighteenth and nineteenth centuries. It is illustrated in Example 23.

EX. 23   BACH - Three-Part Invention No. 3

An interesting point in connection with sequence is that it often justifies the use of some unusual feature which, if stated only once, might sound improbable and accidental. The immediate corroboration not only assures the ear that the unexpected feature was intentional, but creates a pattern that gives point and logic to the music. For instance, in Example 24 the upward leap of a 7th with an unexpectedly long value on the top note is entirely convincing because of its confirmation in the sequence.

EX. 24   BACH - W. T. C., Vol. I, Fugue 15

In Example 25, the repetition of pitches in the lower voice would have sounded merely eccentric and awkward if it had occurred only once; as part of the pattern heard here, it is logical and satisfying.

EX. 25   BACH - W. T. C., Vol. I, Fugue 14

However, there is a limit to what sequence will justify. A melodic turn that is actually objectionable rather than merely unusual will not become any more acceptable with repetition. Also, it is important to remember that too many consecutive repetitions of a pattern make for a monotonous and over-obvious effect. As a rule, three or four may be considered a safe limit.

Sequences of the rhythm alone are also possible, but rhythmic corroboration is more often achieved merely by means of a characteristic pattern, such as that of the dotted sixteenth note followed by a thirty-second note in the following:

EX. 26   BACH - W. T. C., Vol. II, Prelude 16

Largo

There must not be too many *different* rhythmic patterns nor too widely divergent values in the melody itself if unity and coherence are to be maintained.

7) Abrupt halts in the rhythmic motion are to be avoided. Where there is a choice between motion on a strong beat and motion on a weak beat, the latter arrangement is generally preferable, so that there will be a sense of

propulsion into the strong beat. For example, ♩ ♫♩ ♫ is norm-

ally more satisfactory than ♫♩ ♫♩ . But this principle must not be

taken too literally, for exceptions are frequently brought about by special considerations in the musical pattern, nor does it apply when there is an-other voice which can maintain the rhythmic flow at points where the first voice pauses.

SUGGESTED ASSIGNMENTS

Page in Workbook

1. *Exercises for correction*   1

2. *Write five melodies (or as many as specified by the instructor) about four to eight measures in length. These should demonstrate various types of melodic curve. Have some melodies in major, some in minor, and use different meter signatures and tempos.*

¶ Two = Voice

Counterpoint

3

In putting together two or more melodic lines to form counterpoint, several conditions must be met if the result is to be successful:
1) Each line must be good in itself.
2) There must be sufficient independence between the voices in terms of rhythm, direction, and intervallic relationships.
3) On the other hand, they must have enough in common, stylistically and otherwise, so that they will fuse into a convincing whole when combined.
4) In this style, the voices must be *primarily* consonant with each other, dissonance being present but in smaller quantities than consonance.
5) The lines must imply a good harmonic succession. At any given point, the ear hears not only the horizontal lines but the vertical result of combining them; these vertical sounds must represent a satisfactory harmonic progression.

Let us go back now and consider each of these points separately.

The first has already been discussed at some length in Chapter 1 and needs no further elaboration here.

INDEPENDENCE BETWEEN THE TWO LINES

Example 1 on the following page shows two melodic lines that are pleasingly independent rhythmically. The motion is well distributed between the voices; when one pauses, the other keeps the rhythm going.

16

EX. 1   BACH - Two-Part Invention No. 9

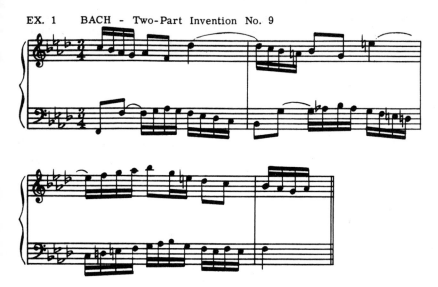

Notice that the respective curves of the two lines here in Example 1 are mostly *dissimilar* in shape, another very important factor in creating independence of feeling.   For one beat at the beginning of the third measure, the voices move not merely in the same direction but in parallel 3rds. Because of the contrary motion employed just before this point, the parallel motion here is agreeable by way of contrast.   If it were continued for very long, however, the effect would be that of a single voice with a parallel harmony part rather than of two independent voices.

Example 2 was written for the purpose of showing the weakness of parallel octaves, which are present at *a* and *b*.   At those points the ear receives the impression that a voice has dropped out, and the feeling of real counterpoint between the voices is lost.

EX. 2

It is for this reason that parallel octaves and unisons between voices are ruled out.   Of course, this principle has nothing to do with the device of

17

doubling a melody an octave higher or lower throughout a passage for the sake of added strength or a particular color—a device that occurs constantly. In such cases the octave doubling is not a real voice but merely a reinforcement of a voice already present.

When an octave moves to a 7th (Example 3*a*) or *vice versa,* the effect is so close to that of parallel octaves as to be objectionable. By the same token, a unison to a 2nd or *vice versa* (Example 3*b*) is too close to a parallel unison to be usable. In fact, approaching the unison by similar motion from *any* interval is weak. As a rule, the octave should not be approached by similar motion (Example 3*c*), although the arrangement at *d,* with the root movement in the lower voice, is good.

EX. 3

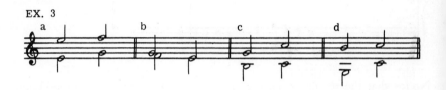

Parallel 5ths are likewise to be avoided, but principally because they imply parallel triads, a device foreign to the style we are using. While this point may therefore not be entirely appropriate under the heading of independence of voices, it can most conveniently be discussed here along with other parallelisms. Any two parallel *perfect* 5ths are poor (Examples 4*a* and *b*), as is the succession of diminished 5th to perfect 5th (at *c*). On the other hand, perfect 5th to diminished 5th is possible if the proper resolution follows (*d*).

EX. 4

These comments on parallelism have involved only counterpoint using note against note (first species). Other situations will be taken up later as they occur in various exercises.

18

UNITY

The third point in our list of requirements, the fact that the voices must have enough in common, is chiefly a matter of stylistic unity. It is perhaps the easiest of the conditions to fulfill.

CONSONANCE VERSUS DISSONANCE

The fourth point concerns the need for a basically consonant style, and obviously involves the question of the intervals used between the voices. It may be helpful, first of all, to consider where the various intervals are found within the major scale (Example 5), and to go over some points of terminology.

EX. 5

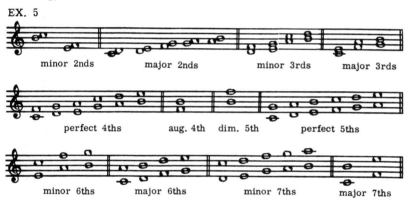

minor 2nds   major 2nds   minor 3rds   major 3rds

perfect 4ths   aug. 4th   dim. 5th   perfect 5ths

minor 6ths   major 6ths   minor 7ths   major 7ths

For purposes of designation, intervals of more than a 10th (and sometimes the 9th and 10th as well) are generally reduced to their simplest terms; for instance, an 11th can be called a 4th, and a 13th can be called a 6th.

An essential interval is one in which both notes belong to the harmony implied. In an unessential interval at least one of the notes is foreign to the harmony (nonharmonic) and then resolves to a harmony note or becomes harmonic itself. Example 6 shows an essential 10th at *a*, an unessential minor 7th at *b* (where the note D is nonharmonic), and an essential 6th at *c*.

EX. 6

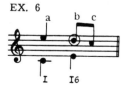

I   I6

Two-Voice Counterpoint

Inasmuch as the terms consonance and dissonance are purely relative and even debatable, a chart is given next to show how intervals (used harmonically) are traditionally classified in the idiom we are concerned with, and also to give some idea of their relative frequency in two-voice counterpoint of the period.

Consonant   *Dissonant*

major 3rd		augmented 4th	fairly frequent; usable principally as
minor 3rd		diminished 5th	essential intervals implying V⁷
major 6th	frequent		
minor 6th			
perfect 8ve			
		major 2nd	
perfect 5th	infrequent	minor 7th	infrequent as essential intervals
		minor 2nd	
		major 7th	very infrequent as essential intervals
		perfect 4th	

It can be seen from this chart that the most usable intervals are the 3rd, 6th, and octave. The octave appears less frequently than the other two, and occurs most often on the tonic note at the beginnings and ends of phrases or sections, occasionally on the dominant note at other points.

Probably the reason for the relatively rare use of the perfect 5th is that it has the bare, incomplete sound of a triad without a third and is a bit stark for this style. When it *is* used, the third of the triad very often precedes or follows shortly. This is the case at the beginning of Example 1.

The "horn 5th" (illustrated in Example 7) involves a particular note-pattern which arose as a result of instrumental practice and became hallowed by traditional usage.

EX. 7   SCARLATTI - Sonata (Longo Ed. No. 5)

This figure was frequently given to the horns in the days when they were valveless and therefore restricted as to the notes they could play.

Notice that the augmented 4th and the diminished 5th occur, in major, only between the leading tone and the fourth scale step, both active tones contained within the dominant seventh harmony. This fact prompted the comment, in the chart above, concerning their use.

The perfect 4th is a special case. Although relatively consonant acoustically, it is classed as a dissonance in this style because of its incomplete and "top-heavy" quality (harsher than that of the perfect 5th), and because its characteristic use on the beat in two-voice baroque counterpoint is that of an unessential interval resolving to a 3rd (Example 8).

EX. 8   BACH - Brandenburg Concerto No. 2

BACH - French Suite No. 2 (Minuet)

Another point against the use of the perfect 4th as an essential interval is that it tends to suggest $^6_4$ chords (triads in second inversion) at points where they would be inappropriate. More will be said about the $^6_4$ chord presently. While the 4th can seldom be employed essentially in note-for-note counterpoint, in other species of counterpoint it occasionally occurs essentially on a weak beat in a fast tempo or with a short time value (Example 9; also the last beat of Example 8b).

EX. 9   BACH - Two-Part Inventions

In minor, additional harmonic intervals occur, notably the augmented 2nd and the diminished 7th, between the natural sixth scale step and the raised seventh step. These intervals can seldom be used in note-for-note counterpoint because of the intervals to which they would normally resolve, a perfect 4th and a perfect 5th, respectively.

Nonharmonic tones (especially of the accented variety) and chromaticism increase the degree of dissonance in music and might therefore be appropriately discussed under this heading. However, discussion of them is being reserved for the next chapter in order that they can be related more directly to the first exercises which actually make use of them.

HARMONIC IMPLICATIONS

The fifth point in our list dealt with the harmonic background implied in counterpoint. Students sometimes find it hard to believe that such a background is invariably present in music of this style; but a careful examination of the works of the great eighteenth- and nineteenth-century contrapuntists will prove it to be true. In writing counterpoint, then, we must make sure that the implied harmonic successions are good; progressions that would be avoided in four-voice harmony must also be avoided here. For example, both of the following are poor because of the harmonies implied.

EX. 10

If the IV chord in Example 10*a* were in first inversion, the implied progression would be entirely acceptable. Similarly, the progression at *b* would be good if the I chord were in second inversion.

Remember that the III₆ and the VI₆ are usable only as passing sounds with the bass moving stepwise. Example 11 illustrates this use in connection with the III₆.

EX. 11   BACH - Brandenburg Concerto No. 5

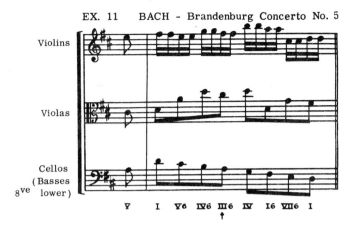

In four-part harmony with harmonic changes on each beat or on every other beat, a static effect results if the bass is held over or repeated from a weak beat to a strong beat (particularly over the bar line). The equivalent of this in two-voice counterpoint is shown in Example 12*a*. Even the retention of *harmony* "from weak to strong" with a change of bass gives a slightly static, though much less objectionable, effect (*b*).

EX. 12

In two-voice counterpoint the bottom voice tends to sound like a real bass, that is, like the bottom voice in an actual harmonization. Consequently, whenever the fifth of a triad appears in the lower voice, an implied second inversion results. The $^6_4$ chord is entirely usable in this style under certain conditions (which should be familiar to the student through his study of harmony); but it is important to remember that the bass of a triad in second inversion should not be approached or left by leap except in a cadence (II I$^6_4$), or in chord repetition. If the $^6_4$ chord is not involved in one of these uses, it must be treated as a passing sound with the bass moving stepwise. Example 13 shows good and bad ways of using the implied $^6_4$ in two-voice counterpoint.

23

EX. 13

The chords II_4^6, III_4^6, and VI_4^6 are of almost no practical use in this style and should ordinarily not be suggested in contrapuntal writing. Notice that if the principles given here are adhered to, two $\frac{6}{4}$ chords will never appear in succession.

CHOICE OF CHORD TONES

In two-voice counterpoint it is obviously impossible to have all three tones of a triad sounded simultaneously. Of course they can sometimes be outlined in succession, but that possibility is not always available. The question then arises: which chord member should be omitted? If we experiment, using a C major triad, we find that omitting the root deprives the chord of its basic identity, and that the E and G might now be construed as root and third of an E minor triad. It appears, then, that the root must ordinarily be present. If we omit the third , it is impossible to tell whether the triad is major or minor; its color factor is conspicuously missing. Moreover, as was previously pointed out, the open 5th is used sparingly in this style, as it tends to suggest the starkness of organum. We conclude, therefore, that the third of the chord is a highly necessary member. If we omit the fifth , the effect is satisfactory. It might be argued that C and E could be heard as third and fifth of an A minor triad. If the chord or key of A minor had been heard

24

just previously, that might be true; otherwise the ear would probably choose the interpretation in which the bottom note is heard as root. In Example 14 no chord fifths are present, yet all the harmonies implied are perfectly clear.

EX. 14

Of course if the fifth scale degree appears in a given melody and the tonic harmony seems called for, either the root or the third will have to be omitted, most often the root. And there are cases in which the chord fifth in the bass with the third in the upper voice is perfectly satisfactory. Examples of these situations are given next, at *a* and *b*, respectively.

EX. 15

DOUBLING

In two-part contrapuntal writing, problems of doubling are obviously not involved as they are in four-part writing. But it might be well to point out the weakness of a doubled third in a prominent position, as at *a* and *b* in the next example. At *b*, the third of the chord happens also to be the leading tone, which makes the doubling of it particularly undesirable.

EX. 16

25

Two-Voice Counterpoint

However, if both voices move stepwise and in contrary motion *through* doublings of this sort, the result is usually acceptable, especially if the doubled note is not on a strong beat (Example 17).

EX. 17

Also, sequences often justify the use of a doubling that might otherwise be questionable.

As a general principle, the rules of doubling that apply in four-voice writing are very often waived for linear reasons, in counterpoint.

SUGGESTED ASSIGNMENTS

	Page in Workbook
1. *Exercises in error detection (1:1)*	3
2. *Be prepared to discuss the requisites of good counterpoint.*	

¶ Exercises in

Two = Voice Counterpoint

4

In counterpoint exercises, one voice is usually given. This is known as the *cantus firmus* * (fixed voice), and that term is often abbreviated to "C. F." Sometimes the C. F. is specified as upper voice, sometimes as lower, and sometimes as middle voice when three voices are present.

When the C. F. is counterpointed with one note in the added voice against each note of the C. F., the result is called "first species" counterpoint. This species can conveniently be designated by the ratio 1:1, said as "one against one." The various species traditionally used in counterpoint study are as follows:

First species: 1:1
Second species: 2:1 and 3:1
Third species: 4:1 and 6:1
Fourth species: Syncopated
Fifth species: Florid (a combination of the other four species)

Even though the approach used in this book is a great deal freer than that of traditional species counterpoint, we shall be working exercises involving the first four of these rhythmic ratios in order to explore the possibilities and problems peculiar to each. The fifth species will not be undertaken as such, since it closely parallels work in free counterpoint to be done.

* The plural is *cantus firmi*. The Italian version, *canto fermo,* is sometimes used instead, in which case the plural is *canti fermi.*

NOTE AGAINST NOTE (1:1)

Most of the rhythmic relationships just mentioned occur frequently in actual music, but the 1:1 ratio is seldom used for long at a time. The reason for this is that it lacks rhythmic independence between voices, one of the characteristics of good counterpoint which has already been discussed. However, it is sometimes employed for a few beats or even a few measures, as in the following excerpts.

EX. 1   BEETHOVEN - Sonata, Op. 13

MOZART - Symphony No. 41, K. 551

In order to illustrate the type of exercise to be done first, let us suppose that we have been given the C. F. shown on the top staff of Example 2 to be used as upper voice. Below it we are to add another voice in 1:1 relationship. One possible counterpoint is shown on the lower staff.

EX. 2

Notice that the vertical or harmonic intervals (those between the voices) here in Example 2 are 3rds (or 10ths), 6ths (or 13ths), and octaves. As pointed out earlier, these are the intervals most used in this style. For the time being, octaves should be employed only on the tonic or dominant notes (the most usual places for them in baroque counterpoint), and chiefly on the tonic at beginnings and endings. The vertical interval of a 5th may appear *occasionally*, preferably surrounded by 3rds or 6ths.

Examples 3, 4, and 5 show frequently encountered faults.

EX. 3

In Example 3 the following bad features can be pointed out:

1) At *a* and *b*, the 5th is a questionable choice as interval.

2) At *b*, there are parallel 5ths.

3) At *c*, the tendency of the leading-tone (G) has been ignored. It should go up to A-flat, not down to E-flat. Furthermore, the bass of the I_4^6 chord should not have been approached by a leap, since the preceding chord is not II and chord repetition is not involved.

4) At *d*, the harmony is carried over from the weak second beat to the strong third beat. Also, the interval of a 4th is poor.

5) At *e*, the leading-tone has been doubled.

6) At *f*, there are parallel octaves.

EX. 4

Here in Example 4 there is too much consecutive use of the same interval, the 6th. The lines lack independence of intervallic distance and of curve. As a general rule, no more than three parallel intervals should be used in succession.

29

EX. 5

In Example 5 the harmonic intervals are not bad, but the lower voice keeps returning to A-flat. Its curve is uninteresting and lacks any strong sense of direction.

In working the exercises assigned in the *Counterpoint Workbook,* in which various rhythmic ratios are to be used, observe the following directions:

1) The same pitch should not be used twice in succession. This would, in effect, give the note double value and would alter the intended rhythmic ratio between the voices.

2) In most cases, the voices should not be more than two octaves apart. Gaps of greater distances may occur briefly now and then. For the time being, the voices should not cross.

3) As a general rule, the bottom voice should be considered a bass—that is, the equivalent of the bottom voice in an actual harmonization. It may, however, occasionally end on the third of the tonic chord in cases where the root does not work out well from a linear standpoint.

4) Chromatic alterations are not to be used in the 1:1 exercises. They may be used beginning with the material on page 13 of the *Workbook.*

(1:1 exercises may be done at this point.)

TWO NOTES AGAINST ONE (2:1)

The exercises to be done next will involve putting two notes in the added voice against each note of the C. F. The example that follows shows a consistent use of the 2:1 relationship.

EX. 6 BEETHOVEN - Sonata, Op. 2, No. 1
(Trio of Minuet)

cresc.   dim.

In 2:1 counterpoint, the notes that occur between the beats (or between the points where the voices coincide) are harmonic in some cases, non-harmonic in others. For instance, in the first measure of Example 6 the second eighth-note in the upper voice is nonharmonic, while the fourth eighth-note is part of the harmony implied at that point. It is also possible to have an unessential (nonharmonic) note *on* the beat, with the essential note following on the second half of the beat. This is the case in the third beat of this first measure; the G is nonharmonic (an accented passing tone), and the A is the essential tone.

Nonharmonic Tones

It may be helpful to review the subject of nonharmonic tones briefly. In Example 7, which gives short illustrations of the various types, the non-harmonic tones are circled. The harmonic background is C major, except where another harmony is indicated.

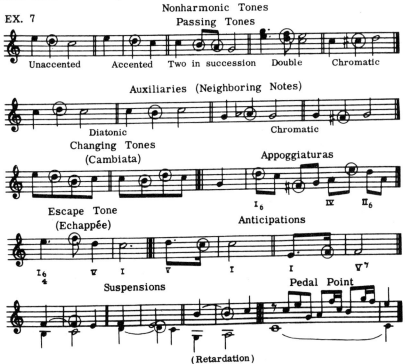

A passing tone is a nonharmonic tone that moves by whole or half step from one harmonic tone to another.

An auxiliary or neighboring tone (or simply neighbor tone) is a non-harmonic tone a whole or half step above or below a harmonic tone. It is approached from the harmonic tone and returns to it.

Changing tones, sometimes known (especially in the first form shown in Example 7) as the *cambiata* figure, are two auxiliaries used in succession. They may or may not be approached from the harmonic tone of which they are neighbors.

An appoggiatura is a nonharmonic tone approached by leap and resolved stepwise, most often in the direction opposite to the leap.*

An escape tone, or échappée, is a nonharmonic tone which, in its most usual form, is approached from a harmonic tone one scale step below, and which then leaps downward to a harmonic tone. The latter is not necessarily a member of the harmony just heard. Much more rarely, the escape tone is approached from a harmonic tone one scale step *above,* and then leaps upward to a harmonic tone.

Example 8 illustrates the use in actual music of the nonharmonic tones defined so far.

EX. 8   BACH - Three-Part Invention No. 12

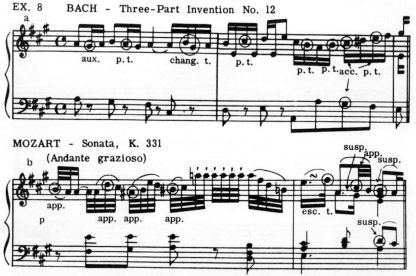

MOZART - Sonata, K. 331

---

* In its most characteristic form the appoggiatura carries a sense of weight or accent, and some theorists insist on this quality as a basic criterion. The author feels that it is more reasonable to allow for an *un*accented type of appoggiatura as well. If this is not done, the unaccented appoggiatura must either be considered an extension of the cambiata figure (which entails certain complications) or given another name. The term "neighbor tone" is reserved for this use in some systems.

MOZART - Sonata, K. 333

The chief point to remember in using these nonharmonic tones is that they must be resolved properly, with the exception of the escape tone, which nearly always appears in one of the patterns shown in Examples 8 *b* and *d*. A fault frequently encountered among students is that of allowing a note which obviously has the function of a passing tone to leap rather than "pass" stepwise.

An anticipation is a nonharmonic tone that occurs just in advance of the harmony to which it belongs. Its most frequent position is in cadences, such as those given in Example 9.

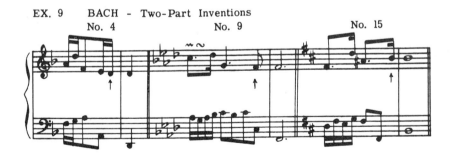

A suspension is a member of one harmony tied over or repeated as a non-harmonic tone in the next, and normally resolved downward into that

33

harmony. Suspensions that resolve upward are sometimes called retardations. The subject of suspensions will be taken up in some detail a little later on in connection with syncopation (pages 53 to 56).

A pedal point is a sustained or repeated note, usually on the tonic or dominant pitch, which lasts through two or more harmonies. Although it is most often seen in the bottom voice (hence its name), it may occur in any voice. It usually begins and ends as a harmonic note, but may, between these points, be dissonant to the harmony—that is, nonharmonic. In Example 10*a* the tonic pedal point appears in both the middle and the bottom voices; one has repeated eighth notes, the other, longer sustained tones. In Example 10*b* the tonic pedal point is part of an eighth-note figure.

EX. 10   HAYDN - Sonata (G. Schirmer Ed. No. 1)

BACH - French Suite No. 1 (Bourrée)

Intervals Between Voices

In 2:1 counterpoint the 3rd, 6th, and octave remain the strongest and most frequent choices for use *on* the beat, and they may appear between beats as well. The intervals of a 2nd, a 7th, and a 4th, which were generally avoided in 1:1 counterpoint, now become acceptable for use *between* beats because of their lighter rhythmic position there, and because the ear hears them merely as sounds connecting the basic 1:1 counterpoint

34

(Examples 11 *a* and *b*). They may also be used *on* the beat as unessential intervals with the essential intervals following (*c*). The numbers between the staves indicate the size of the vertical intervals at those points.

EX. 11   BACH   BACH
a   Two-Part Invention   Two-Part Invention
     No. 9   b   No. 13   c

Similarly, the octave and the 5th, which were used sparingly in 1:1 counterpoint, appear frequently between beats in 2:1. The same applies to certain doublings, such as a doubled third in a primary triad, although even brief doublings of the *leading-tone* are best avoided.

Techniques of Writing 2:1

One way, though not necessarily the best way, of writing 2:1 counterpoint is to start with a 1:1 version and convert it by the addition of notes between the beats, in one voice. Example 12 shows how a 2:1 version might be derived from a 1:1 counterpoint we have used previously. Of course only the top and bottom voices in the example are intended to sound in the 2:1 version.

EX. 12

C. F.

1:1

2:1

35

Various devices for expanding 1:1 counterpoint to 2:1 can be seen in operation here. Probably the easiest and smoothest of these is simply the insertion of a passing tone between two notes originally a 3rd apart, as at *d, e, g*. Sometimes a 4th in the 1:1 version can be filled in with two adjacent passing tones, one of them accented, as at *c*. At the beginning and near the end, the original 1:1 counterpoint moves by step and obviously does not allow for the insertion of a passing-tone (except a chromatic passing-tone, which would not be particularly appropriate in this style). However, a leap to a chord tone can be made instead, as at *a, b,* and *f*. Care must be taken not to overuse this latter device. Too much outlining of chords to the exclusion of stepwise motion becomes tiresome, and tends to make the voice sound less like a line than a succession of harmonic figurations.

A second, and frequently preferable approach to the writing of 2:1 counterpoint is to invent the 2:1 version directly, without having it grow out of a 1:1 version, in which case one major possibility is added: we can have the same note on adjacent *beats* because other notes will intervene, and the notes on the beat will then not be repeated in succession. For example, according to the restrictions that apply in 1:1 counterpoint, we could not write the following because of the repetition at *a* and *b*:

EX. 13

But in 2:1 counterpoint there would be no objection to the following:

EX. 14

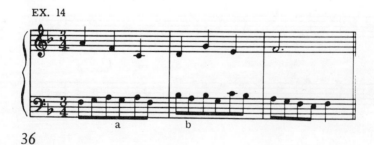

36

In this particular example (14), a lower neighboring tone or auxiliary carries on the eighth-note motion at *a* and *b*. But these notes between the beats might have been chord tones rather than nonharmonic tones if we had happened to choose another counterpoint.

Parallelism

In 1:1 counterpoint, parallel octaves and 5ths are generally apparent to either the ear or the eye. But in 2:1 the presence of intervening notes between the beats makes the situation more complex as far as the recognition of parallelism is concerned. There are even certain note-patterns which are condemned by some writers on counterpoint on the grounds of parallelism but accepted by others. It would seem, then, that the only sensible criterion is what was actually practiced by composers of this period (Bach in particular), and it is this standard on which the comments in Example 15 are based.

EX. 15

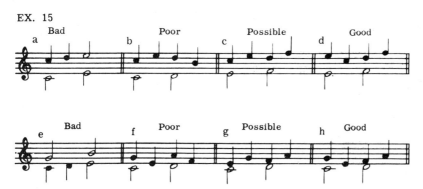

The cases given here in Example 15 can be listed according to the following categories, which may be of some help in remembering which patterns are usable:

1) "open" (with intervening notes in one voice, as in *a* and *e*): bad
2) "symmetrical" or "corresponding"
    a) with parallelism on strong beats, as in *b* and *f*: poor
    b) with parallelism on weak beats, as in *c* and *g*: possible
3) "asymmetrical" (parallel intervals not at corresponding places in the measure, as in *d* and *h*): good

It is obvious, then, that if there are parallel octaves or 5ths in a 1:1 version, the addition of intervening notes in a 2:1 version will not destroy the feeling of parallelism. Also, it is particularly necessary, in converting

37

1:1 to 2:1, to be on guard against parallel octaves that may be formed by the addition of notes (Example 16).

EX. 16

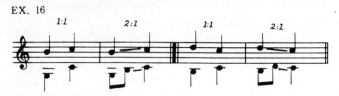

One special case should be mentioned. The consecutive 5ths illustrated in the next example are not considered objectionable, since the second of the two is nonessential. They may therefore be used freely.

EX. 17   SCARLATTI - Sonata (Longo Ed. No. 5)

(Diatonic 2:1 exercises may be done at this point.)

CHROMATICISM

Chromaticism may be a melodic element or a harmonic element, or both at the same time. Used purely melodically, it takes the form of nonharmonic tones, such as those seen earlier in Examples 7 and 8. In such cases the harmonic background is of course not affected by the chromaticism.

In Example 18, on the other hand, the chromatically altered notes are part of the harmony.

EX. 18   BACH - French Suite No. 1 (Allemande)

The altered chords implied here are "secondary dominants." These are chords which stand in the relationship of dominant to a diatonic chord. This device is an extremely frequent one in baroque music as well as in music of a later day, and it may be used in connection with any of the diatonic triads. Another basically dominant harmony which often performs the same function is the VII[7] (or incomplete V[9]) of each diatonic chord. With certain chords this is a diminished seventh sound, with others (IV and V), its natural form is a half-diminished seventh, though it may be altered to the diminished form. The harmonic progressions involved in these possibilities are shown in Example 19.

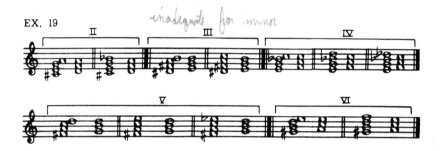

EX. 19

Example 20 illustrates the use of the VII[7] as a dominant embellishing chord.

EX. 20   BACH - Two-Part Invention No. 6

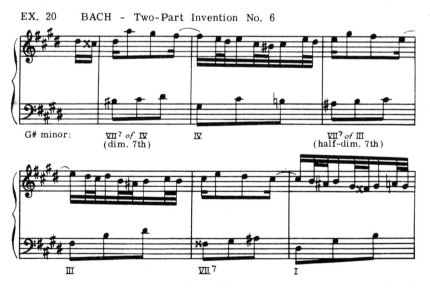

G# minor: VII[7] of IV   IV   VII[7] of III
              (dim. 7th)   (half-dim. 7th)

III   VII[7]   I

39

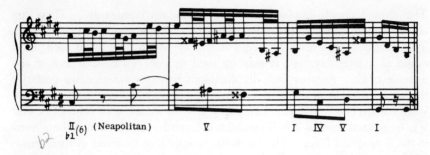

II(6) (Neapolitan)   V   I   IV   V   I
b1

Besides these secondary dominant forms, many other altered harmonies appear in the style we are studying. A complete catalogue of these is neither appropriate nor possible here, but it would include the Neapolitan 6th, which was seen in Example 20 and which is quite common in music of the baroque period, and also the augmented 6th chords, which are rare, though much used later on in the classical period. The harmonic background of Example 21*a* includes several altered chords, among them a French 6th, though in an uncharacteristic inversion. A German 6th is outlined in Example 21*b*.

EX. 21   BACH - W. T. C., Vol. II, Prelude 12

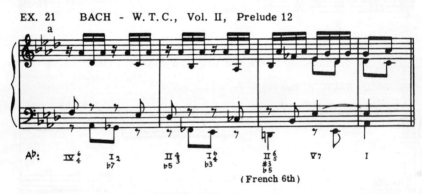

Ab: IV 6/4   I 4/2   II 4/3   I 6/4   II 6/5   V7   I
             b7   b5 3   b3   #3 b5
                                              (French 6th)

MOZART - Sonata, K. 330
b Andante cantabile

German 6th

Another chromatic device, change of mode, is illustrated in the last half of the second measure of Example 21*a*. At that point A-flat *minor* is substituted for the expected A-flat major (that is, C-flat for C-natural).

It might be mentioned that Bach frequently makes use of a chromatically descending bass, especially in minor. Two instances of this device are seen in *a* and *b* of Example 22. The position of the voices is reversed in the second measure of *b*, so that the chromatically descending line appears in the top voice.

EX. 22   BACH - Three-Part Invention No. 9

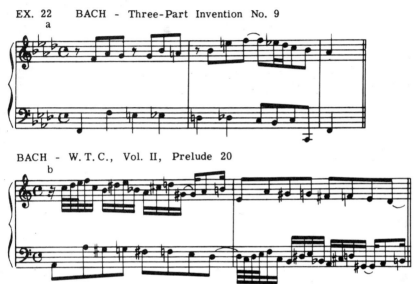

BACH - W. T. C., Vol. II, Prelude 20

Both these excerpts provide excellent illustrations of characteristic Bach treatment of chromaticism and nonharmonic tones. The works quoted should be carefully examined in their entirety.

In the examples of chromaticism shown so far, the altered chords operated within a given key. But they may also be used to effect modulation, the new key being established through cadential treatment. This is the case in the following.

EX. 23   BACH - French Suite No. 1 (Polonaise)

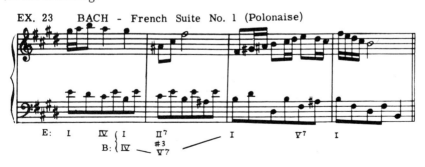

Exercises in Two-Voice Counterpoint

In two-voice counterpoint, chromaticism may be present in either voice or in both voices at once. The former arrangement is the more usual and ordinarily the stronger in this style. When two chromatic alterations occur at once, both may be harmonic, both may be melodic, or, as in the next example, one may be melodic, the other harmonic.

EX. 24   BEETHOVEN - Sonata, Op. 22

As a rule, chromatic alteration of a tone is best introduced in the voice that has just had that tone (Example 25*a*). Otherwise a cross relation (*b*) results. Even when other notes intervene between the beats (*c* and *d*) the effect is poor, and such cross relations should be avoided. The arrangement at *e* is not considered a cross relation; it merely involves an octave doubling of the tone that is to be chromatically changed.

EX. 25

However, cross relations that result from the simultaneous use of the ascending and descending forms of the melodic minor scale are common in this style and are generally acceptable (Example 26).

EX. 26   BACH - Three-Part Invention No. 1

42

A few reminders on chromatic spelling may not be amiss here. In an ascending chromatic passage the chromatic note is normally spelled as the raised form of the preceding diatonic note (for example, C, C-sharp, D), in a descending passage as the lowered form of the preceding diatonic note (D, D-flat, C). The ascending and descending forms of a chromatic scale in C would therefore be spelled as follows:

EX. 27

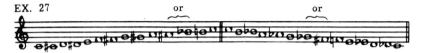

Two exceptions can be seen here. The raised sixth scale step may be spelled as the lowered seventh step instead, when that spelling conforms with the harmonic background. For the same reason, the raised-fourth spelling is very often substituted for the lowered-fifth spelling in descending chromatic passages. Notice that we do not normally raise the third and seventh scale steps in major, since in each case there is an actual scale tone a half-step above, which can more properly be used. By the same token, the first and fourth scale steps are almost never lowered chromatically.

In a chromatic line that reverses direction, the ultimate destination of the chromatically altered note determines how it shall be spelled. This point is illustrated in Example 28.

EX. 28

SUGGESTED ASSIGNMENTS

		Page in Workbook
1.	1:1 exercises, major	5
2.	1:1 exercises, minor	7
3.	Exercises in error detection (1:1, 2:1, 3:1, 4:1)	9
4.	2:1 exercises, diatonic	11
5.	2:1 exercises, with chromatic alterations	13

⟨ *Exercises in* Two =Voice *Counterpoint* (*Concluded*)

5

THREE NOTES AGAINST ONE (3:1)

Example 1 shows excerpts that demonstrate the 3:1 ratio. Incidentally, *c* is also a good example of invertible counterpoint, a device which will be discussed later.

EX. 1   BACH - W. T. C., Vol. II, Fugue 6
a

BUXTEHUDE - Fugue in C major (Organ)
b

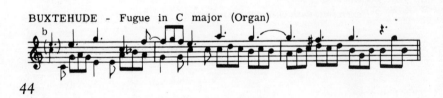

44

BEETHOVEN - Sonata, Op. 2, No. 3

The process of writing 3:1 counterpoint is essentially the same as that of writing the 2:1 variety. The chief difference, encountered especially if one is working from a 1:1 basis, is the fact that with an additional note between beats, the relationship between note patterns and interval span changes. For example, in 2:1 the interval of a 3rd could very easily be filled in with a passing-tone, but it must be treated in some other way in 3:1, while the 4th becomes the interval most conveniently filled in with passing-tones.

Example 2 shows some of the melodic possibilities in 3:1, arranged by basic interval. Since it is possible to have the same note on succeeding beats with other notes intervening, we have at our disposal certain patterns in which the line returns to the note it left on the preceding beat. Some of these are given first, after which are shown a few of the many patterns possible in spanning each interval (up to a 5th) with three notes. Descending intervals happened to be chosen for purposes of illustration here and in Example 7, but the same general principles apply in the case of ascending intervals. Of course the melodic figures in each line do not all involve the same harmonic background, and the choice of figure will depend in part on the harmony implied.

EX. 2
Basic melodic
interval

45

This list and others to follow are offered, not in a spirit of scientific cataloguing, but rather to suggest some of the many patterns which can successfully be used in the exercises. Remember that it is unwise to use too many *different* patterns in one exercise. This is not to say that the same melodic figure should be repeated from beginning to end, but rather that a greater sense of unity can be gained if there is some economy in the use of figures.

Avoid stepwise motion followed by a leap in the same direction (Examples 3a and b). An exception is the pattern shown at c, which is possible. Repeated notes are still ruled out, even between the last note of one group of three and the first note of the next group (d). In actual music this last arrangement is seldom used except in a sequential pattern. Also to be avoided is the type of line shown at e, which turns back over the same notes repeatedly and lacks a sense of direction. Be sure not to leap from nonharmonic tones that should be resolved stepwise (f).

EX. 3

As for parallelism in 3:1, the principles discussed in the section on 2:1 apply. A good general rule is to avoid parallel octaves or 5ths between any part of a beat and the first note of the next beat (Example 4).

EX. 4

Exercises in Two-Voice Counterpoint (Concluded)

For purposes of illustration the 1:1 counterpoint from Example 2 in Chapter 4, page 28, has been used again in Example 5, as the basis for a satisfactory 3:1 version. Here, again, only the top and bottom voices are intended to sound in the 3:1 version.

EX. 5

It should perhaps be stressed that the writing of 3:1 counterpoint (as of 2:1 and 4:1) need not be approached from a 1:1 basis. Although that is generally a *safe* method, it involves unnecessary limitations and does not always produce the most imaginative and interesting results.

(3:1 exercises may be done at this point.)

FOUR NOTES AGAINST ONE (4:1)

The excerpts in Example 6 illustrate the use of the 4:1 relationship in music. Compare *c* with Example 1*a* in Chapter 4, page 28, which stated the same theme in 1:1 fashion.

EX. 6   MOZART - Piano Sonata, K. 498a

BACH - W. T. C., Vol. I Prelude 5

EX. 6   BEETHOVEN - Sonata, Op. 13 (Pathétique)

Some of the patterns possible in 4:1 counterpoint are arranged by basic interval and shown in Example 7.

EX. 7

These patterns involve the devices we have used before in 2:1 and 3:1—passing tones, auxiliaries, escape tones, appoggiaturas, and leaps to another chord tone. In 4:1 there is a sense of slightly greater weight on the first and third notes of the group of four. Consequently these are frequently harmonic tones, the second and fourth notes being nonharmonic. Other arrangements are of course possible and quite common. In any case, all four notes of a group generally center around a single harmony; that is, the harmonic rhythm in 4:1 normally involves only one chord to a beat. Occasionally the harmony may change once within the beat if necessary, but attempts to imply more than two harmonies to a beat are generally unmusical and awkward.

Patterns to be avoided are shown in Example 8.

EX. 8

Stepwise motion followed by a leap in the same direction is particularly poor in 4:1, and especially when it occurs between the last note of one

49

group and the first note of the next, as in Examples 8*a* and *b*. At *c* a nonharmonic tone which should resolve stepwise leaps instead. The figures at *d* and *e* are ruled out in these exercises because of the repetition which would destroy the basic ratio. In actual music however, they would be acceptable if used in *sequential* fashion—not merely in isolated instances.

Parallel octaves and 5ths between part of one beat and the beginning of the next beat are to be avoided, with one exception: those between the *second* note of a group of four and the first note of the next group. Example 9 illustrates this point.

EX. 9

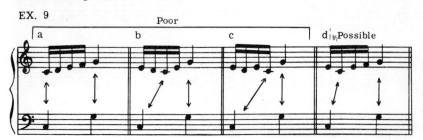

An example of satisfactory 4:1 counterpoint derived from a 1:1 version is illustrated in the following elaboration of Example 2 on page 28.

EX. 10

(4:1 exercises may be done at this point.)

FOURTH SPECIES (SYNCOPATED)

Fourth species counterpoint involves the sort of rhythmic relationship seen in the following excerpts.

50

EX. 11   BACH - Two-Part Invention No. 6

a

BEETHOVEN - Sonata, Op. 13 (Pathétique)

b   Allegro

HAYDN - Andante con Variazioni

Andante con moto

c   d

It can easily be seen that this kind of arrangement involves a 1:1 counter-point with one of the voices shifted half a beat ahead. The excerpts in Examples 11*a, b,* and *c* are based on the following 1:1 relationships:

EX. 12

a   b   c

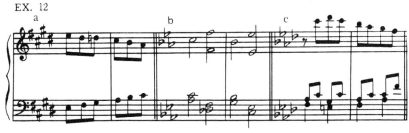

But this is not to say that all 1:1 counterpoint can be converted to good fourth species counterpoint by shifting one of the voices; certain patterns in 1:1 lend themselves well to the shifting process, others do not. When the shifted note fits into the harmony (Examples 13a and b) or forms a suspension (c and d), the effect is generally good.

EX. 13

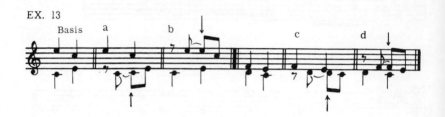

Anticipations, though likely to be less successful than suspensions, are sometimes possible. Example 14 shows the anticipations that would have resulted if the top voice in the E major Invention had been shifted in the other direction.

EX. 14

(Tied sixteenth notes rather than off-beat eighths have been used in the notation here, so that the vertical intervals on each beat can be seen more clearly.) Obviously the effect of these anticipations is less pleasing than that of the suspensions in the passage as Bach wrote it. Anticipations do appear later in the invention, however, and can be seen in the example quoted in Chapter 4, page 39.

If the shifting of a voice produces results other than those just mentioned, it is likely to be unsatisfactory. Consider, for instance, the poor effect that would result if the lower voice in the passage from the E major Invention were delayed by half a beat. This is shown in Example 15.

EX. 15

The difficulty here is that the shifting process creates certain retardations which cannot be successfully used.

Inasmuch as the suspension is the most frequent and effective device in syncopated counterpoint, some special consideration of it seems in order here.

The Suspension

Example 16 shows some possibilities in suspensions. Below each are figures which refer to the intervals involved and which are used in describing the suspension. For instance, we speak of a "4–3 suspension" or a "9–8 suspension."

EX. 16

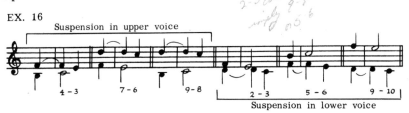

Of course these may be used on other scale steps as well. The suspended note may be either tied (as here) or repeated; the presence or absence of a tie does not affect its function as a suspension. Occasionally, the tied note or the repeated note is replaced by a rest. This happens consistently in Example 11c. The effect to the ear, harmonically speaking, is generally the same.

There are certain suspensions that should be avoided:

EX. 17

53

The 2–1 suspension at *a* (Example 17) is awkward because the note of resolution is heard along with the suspended note. Those at *b, c, d,* and *e* are generally unsatisfactory in two-voice counterpoint because of the resolution to essential 4ths and 5ths. With a third voice taking certain other notes, these would be usable. The 7–8 suspension at *f* is traditionally avoided in academic counterpoint because of the irregular resolution of the interval of a 7th, with the bottom note moving down. However, this prohibition does not seem to be entirely supported by the practice of eighteenth-century composers, some of whom did not hesitate to use the 7–8 suspension.

Suspensions do not always resolve directly; the resolution may be delayed by the insertion of one or more notes between the suspended note and the note of resolution (Example 18).

EX. 18   BACH - Two-Part Invention No. 3

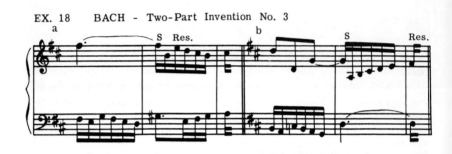

W. T. C., Vol. I, Fugue 22

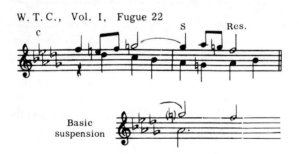

In *c* of this last example the suspended note moves upward briefly before resolving downward to F. Such cases must not be mistaken for retardations, in which the true resolution is upward.

Sometimes the resolutions of suspensions are ornamented, as in the excerpts shown in Example 19.

Exercises in Two-Voice Counterpoint (Concluded)

EX. 19   BACH - W. T. C., Vol. I, Fugue 17

W. T. C., Vol. I, Fugue 8

Example 11a made use of several suspensions in a row, a device known as a "chain suspension." The chain principle is most often applied to a series of suspensions based on parallel 3rds:

EX. 20   Chain Suspension   Basis

Eighth-note suspensions, the quarter note being the unit, may occur on any beat (see Example 20a). Quarter-note suspensions should occur only on strong beats (Example 21a). The preparatory note should be consonant and should be at least as long as the suspended note itself (Example 21b).

EX. 21

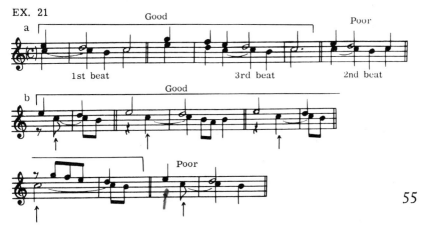

55

Exercises in Two-Voice Counterpoint (Concluded)

Two further possibilities, those of changing the harmony and of letting voices move to other chord members as the resolution of a suspension takes place, will be discussed later in the section on the suspension in three-voice writing. They should not be employed in our present work.

Other Aspects of Fourth-Species Counterpoint

In fourth-species counterpoint, syncopated parallel 5ths and octaves are avoided just as simultaneous 5ths and octaves are in 1:1 counterpoint (Example 22).

EX. 22

Ties (or repetition) between the last fraction of one beat and the beginning of the next are sometimes used in forming rhythms of three and four. Example 23a shows an excerpt involving a triplet rhythm with ties between groups, while b shows the 2:1 basis of the upper voice. Since this basis involves ties and suspensions within itself, it may be still further reduced to a 1:1 form (c).

EX. 23   BACH - W. T. C., Vol. I, Prelude 13

A continued use of ties between groups of four (sixteenth notes when the quarter note is the unit) is rare in this style, probably because it produces a halting effect at the points where the ties interrupt the decided motion of the preceding notes. In the next example, repetition of notes rather than ties is involved.

EX. 24   BACH - W. T. C., Vol. II, Prelude 12

Example 24 also illustrates the inclusion of suspensions within an arpeggiated harmonic pattern. The chords which form the basis of the pattern in this case are given below the example so that the suspensions can be seen more clearly.

We have found that very uneven results were obtained when a 1:1 counterpoint was converted to a syncopated version by shifting one of the voices forward half a beat. This process was successful only when the shifted note was part of the new harmony or formed a suspension or an anticipation. The same is true of attempts to convert 2:1 or 3:1 counterpoint to versions involving groups of three or four by tying or repeating the last note of each group so that it becomes the first note of the next group as well. This approach is therefore not recommended. Counterpoint using the sort of rhythmic relationships seen in Examples 23 and 24 is best written directly.

(Exercises on the suspension, using two voices, may be done at this point.)

RHYTHMIC ACTIVITY DIVIDED BETWEEN THE VOICES

In all the exercises done so far, except those in 1:1, one of the voices carried the burden of rhythmic activity while the other moved in longer values.

It is possible, however, to convert a 1:1 version to 2:1, 3:1, or 4:1 with the rhythmic activity distributed between the two voices as desired. Example 25 demonstrates this process.

EX. 25

The rhythmic motion may be carried through to the last strong beat as in version *b*, or simply stopped in both voices at the beginning of the last measure, as in the other versions. Though the motion alternates between the voices, the alternation must not occur with mathematical regularity or the effect will be stilted and monotonous. Notice that at times *both* voices move at once. Ordinarily a cessation of motion in both voices at the same time gives a static and undesirable effect. This is particularly true on weak beats of the measure, but an occasional *brief* slackening of the motion is quite acceptable—for example, ♩. ♪ rather than ♫♫ or ♫♩ rather than ♫♫ .

While the rhythms ♩. ♪ and ♫♩ are highly usable, the opposites of these, ♪ ♩. and ♫♪. , are uncharacteristic of the style and should be avoided. The same is generally true of ♫♩ , though it might conceivably be used in a sequential pattern at a moderate tempo, with another voice filling in the rhythmic pulse on the third sixteenth. The pattern ♫♫ , with the quarter note as the unit, has a tendency to sound a bit stiff and square-cut if preceded by notes of longer value—for example, ♩ ♫♫ or ♫ ♫♫ . On the other hand, the rhythms ♫♩♫♫ and ♫♫♫♫ are good and entirely usable. In any case, a tie from the last note of this figure into the next beat is usually effective: ♫♫ ♫♫♫ .

58

Exercises in Two-Voice Counterpoint (Concluded)

or ♫♪ ♪♫ or ♫♪ ♫ .

It is normally weak to tie a note to another note of longer value. Thus, patterns such as ♫♫♪ and ♪♫♪ are to be avoided.

Rests of short duration may sometimes be employed, principally at the beginnings of exercises.

SUGGESTED ASSIGNMENTS

	Page in Workbook
1. 3:1 exercises	15–17
2. 4:1 exercises	19–23
3. Comprehensive exercise (1:1, 2:1, 3:1, 4:1)	25
4. Exercises in fourth species (syncopated) counterpoint	27
5. Exercises on suspensions (two voices)	27–29
6. Exercises in converting 1:1 counterpoint to other rhythms, with the motion distributed between the voices	31

¶ Motive Development
and the Two = Part Invention

6

THE MOTIVE

The term *motive* has been defined in various ways. By some it is considered the equivalent of a *figure*, or the smallest possible unit in a melodic phrase. To others it signifies a melodic statement of somewhat greater length, often one or two measures, though seldom more than four. This latter interpretation is the one which we shall adopt.

Much could be written about the possibilities in motive construction and treatment—the fact that the motive may consist of smaller figures repeated sequentially, or that such repetition may not be involved; that it should have some distinctive or striking feature that makes it interesting and easily recognizable in subsequent statements; that it may start on the beat or with an anacrusis; that it may be first presented alone or be accompanied by another voice; and so on. These, and many other points can be observed as we examine portions of the Bach inventions, and as the student does further analysis of other contrapuntal music as part of his assigned work.

J. S. Bach wrote fifteen two-voice compositions called *Inventionen* and fifteen three-voice works which he called *Symphonien*, both sets for the clavier. These are now generally known as the *Two-Part Inventions* and the *Three-Part Inventions*. The term "part" here is of course equivalent to "voice," and has nothing to do with form as it does when used in connection with the "Part-forms."

Motive Development and the Two-Part Invention

CONSTRUCTION AND CONTENT

An invention may be described as a short contrapuntal work, generally sectional in form, in which a motive is announced at the beginning and developed imitatively. The most usual plan for the beginning of a two-part invention is shown in Example 1.

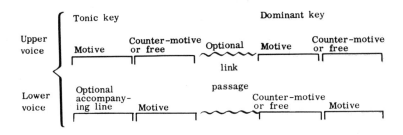

A counter-motive is a melodic line that normally appears first against the second announcement of the motive, is present during the remainder of the opening section, and recurs later in the invention. The term counter-motive has not been previously used, to the author's knowledge, but it has been adopted here because it parallels the term "counter-subject," which describes a voice with a very similar function in fugue; also it seems preferable to "fixed counterpoint" and "contrapuntal associate," both of which have been used to mean the same thing. If the melodic line that accompanies the second statement of the motive does *not* return consistently, it is called simply "free material."

Link passages between the first pair of statements and the second pair are infrequent. This type of transitional passage and the retransition to the tonic that often occurs between the second and third statements of the motive in a three-part invention are both called "codetta" in some counterpoint books. However, since that name is normally applied to a short passage added at the end of a section to round it off, it seems inappropriate for a passage the main function of which is to lead from one section to another.

After its initial statements, such as those plotted in Example 1, the motive reappears in different keys, now in one voice and now in another, preferably with some interesting changes, additions, or deletions. In these announcements Bach usually confines himself to the five most closely related keys:

In major or minor	In major	In minor
Dominant	Supertonic	Subtonic (whole
Subdominant		step below the
Mediant		tonic)
Submediant		

These statements are often separated by "episodes," which are short intermediate sections in which the motive does not appear intact, though *portions* of it are very likely to be employed. In analyzing such passages, the term "motive-element" may prove useful. At the end of the invention, the motive is normally announced once or twice in the home key. The composition as a whole generally falls into at least two or three clearly defined sections, the end of each usually being marked by a definite cadence.

DEVELOPMENT THROUGH SPECIAL DEVICES

In any case this is only a general plan. The content of each invention is determined chiefly by the nature of the motive and its inherent possibilities for development. Some of these are demonstrated next, with a motivic fragment for purposes of simplicity.

EX. 2

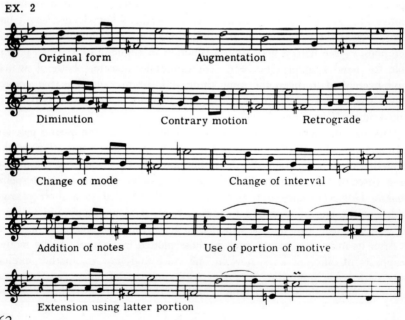

62

Stretto

Contrary motion is often referred to as inversion. However, for purposes of clarity, the term inversion will be reserved in this book for the exchanging of position by voices in invertible counterpoint. This is discussed in Chapter 11.

The three devices in Example 2 that figure most often in the Bach inventions are the use of a portion of the motive, extension of the motive by sequential repetition, and *stretto*. The term stretto, meaning "tight" in Italian, is applied to the sort of telescoped arrangement shown at the end of Example 2, presumably because the two statements are pulled tightly together instead of being spread out consecutively. Diminution, augmentation, and contrary motion occur now and then, the last two in the two-part invention quoted in Example 3 on page 64. In general, however, they are more characteristic of larger contrapuntal forms such as the fugue. Retrograde (sometimes described by the term *cancrizans,* the Latin word for crab) is rare in music. Not only is it difficult to write, but the average ear has trouble in recognizing a melodic line when it is played backwards, the point of the device thereby being lost. A combination of two or more of these processes is quite possible, such as augmentation and contrary motion (see Example 15, Chapter 9, page 107). It might be added parenthetically that these devices, both singly and in combination, figure constantly in much twelve-tone music.

The fact that they are all listed here together should not be construed as a suggestion that they be used *en masse.* Some will be successful with a particular motive, while others would be forced and unnatural. In other words, the use of any of them should be suggested by the music itself rather than be imposed arbitrarily.

ANALYSIS OF INVENTIONS

It is assumed that all counterpoint students will do some analysis of the Bach inventions as part of their assigned work. By way of preparation,

63

some excerpts from certain two-part inventions will be given and discussed. First it is necessary to say something about the terms and symbols to be used. The word motive has already been mentioned. Remember that this word is usually employed rather than "theme" in speaking about the chief melodic idea in an invention. For convenience, "M." may be used in designating the appearances of the motive and "C.M." the appearances of the counter-motive. If, as happens very rarely, a second motive is involved, the two motives may be labeled "M.I." and "M.II." Free material may simply be left unlabeled, or the word "Free" may be written in. For the extension of a musical idea, use a wavy line. For material that is related to or derived from some foregoing element, but not close enough to it to be analyzed as the same, use a dotted line plus an indication such as "(M.)" or "(C.M.)" to show the derivation of the material. Brackets (⌐⌐) are helpful in showing the extent of each musical element. Pronounced cadences at the end of sections and the key in which each occurs should also be indicated—for example, "Cad., (rel. minor)."

First of all, let us examine the beginning of the first Two-Part Invention. Example 3 shows only six measures out of a total of twenty-two.

EX. 3   BACH - Two-Part Invention No. 1

The motive in this case is only half a measure long and begins on the tonic note after a sixteenth rest. It is imitated an octave lower by the left hand in the second half of the measure while the right hand plays a counter-motive which is necessarily brief here. With longer motives the counter-motive may develop into a more important and striking line. Next, the motive is announced in the upper voice in the dominant. (Although the lower voice drops out in this invention, in the majority of the other inventions it continues, taking the counter-motive or free material.) Then there follows an imitation of the motive by the lower voice, in the dominant, an octave below the preceding announcement. One interval at the end of the motive is changed from a 5th to a 4th to fit the harmonic scheme. This is also the case later on in measure 5.

Next comes a sequential series of announcements in the upper voice with the motive in contrary motion, while the lower voice takes an augmented version of the beginning of the motive. This is followed in measure 5 by a statement of the motive in its original rhythm and direction on the supertonic (V of V). In the first half of measure 6 both voices are extended, the upper one by sequential treatment of a portion of the motive. The last half of the measure is devoted to bringing about a strong cadence in the dominant key. If we were to analyze the rest of the invention we would find that contrary motion continues to be used very frequently. This is the only one of the Bach inventions that makes such extensive use of that device.

Notice that in this invention, as in most, there is no break between the motive and the material that follows. One flows smoothly into the other. In certain inventions it is even difficult to know exactly where one ends and the other begins. Therefore it may be necessary in analysis to count a particular note as both the last note of the motive and the first note of the counter-motive or free material.

The motive may begin in the second voice immediately after the last note of the motive in the first voice, or along with the last note, or even one or two notes before it—so that the motive overlaps itself briefly. An analysis of more extensive overlapping is usually not warranted, except in cases where an actual canonic treatment is used, as in Numbers 2 and 8 of Bach's *Two-Part Inventions*. Canons will be discussed in Chapter 9.

The beginning of Invention Number 8 is shown next. The two voices there have the same material, but one begins a measure sooner than the other. Later in the invention the canonic treatment is dropped, and the construction is similar to that in the other inventions.

EX. 4   BACH - Two-Part Invention No. 8

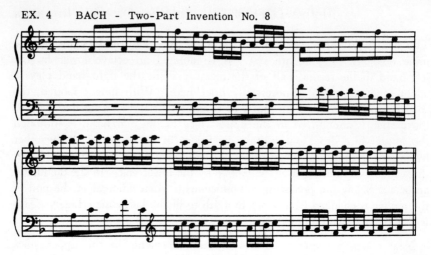

In Invention Number 1 (Example 3) and in others, the motive is announced alone at the start. Sometimes, however, it is accompanied by another voice. This is most likely to happen when the motive begins on a note other than the tonic. The second voice can then take the tonic note at the beginning, thereby establishing the key more definitely. It may also be useful as a bass which helps to define the harmonic implications in the course of the motive. At other times it may serve to keep the rhythm going where the motive has a note of longer value. All three functions are demonstrated in Examples 5 and 6.

In some cases this added voice is actually the counter-motive, which appears again in the other voice against the motive, and presumably elsewhere in the invention (Example 5). Incidentally, the motive in Example 5 is one of the longest to be found in the Bach inventions.

EX. 5   BACH - Two-Part Invention No. 9

Instead of being an actual counter-motive, the added voice at the start may simply be free material, usually without much sense of linear importance, that never recurs in the course of the invention. This arrangement is seen in Invention Number 15:

EX. 6   BACH - Two-Part Invention No. 15

Motive Development and the Two-Part Invention

This same excerpt (Example 6) can serve as an illustration of two other points. First, notice that the initial imitation of the motive, in the third measure, is in the *dominant* key, whereas the more usual plan calls for the tonic at that point. Four others of the Bach two-part inventions (Numbers 5, 10, 12, and 14) are similar in this respect.

Second, note that in measure 5 the motive appears just after the *third* beat of the measure, whereas originally it came just after the first beat. Such shifting of the place of the motive in the measure is normally permissible only from the first beat to the third beat, or from the second beat to the fourth beat of a measure of four beats—not from the first beat to the second or fourth beat. In a three-beat measure, no shifting from one beat to another should take place. This statement concerns chiefly the first announcements of the motive and does not apply in strettos.

Occasionally the counter-motive assumes such importance that it is almost on a par with the motive. For instance in *Two-Part Invention Number 6* (E major), the beginning of which was quoted in Example 11a in Chapter 5, page 51, the two lines are presented together at the start, work together in harness so consistently, and are so similar and so equal in importance, that it is hard to know which one should be called the motive. Probably the most logical analysis is to consider them two coordinate motives.

The introduction of a second motive is one further possibility that might be mentioned. *Two-Part Invention Number 13* seems to require such an analysis because of the prominent idea that appears in the upper voice in measure 3, and figures importantly throughout.

EX. 7   BACH - Two-Part Invention No. 13

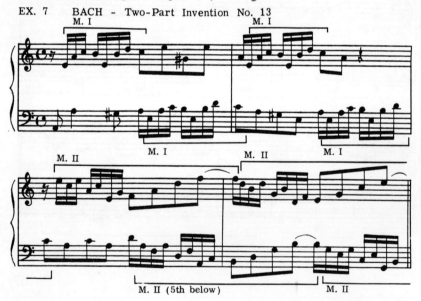

An analysis involving overlapping voices forming a brief canon at the 5th below seems indicated in the case of the second motive.

Example 8 shows an entire two-part invention with analytical markings added. In cases such as this, where there is no counter-motive, a bracket alone (without "M.") is sufficient to identify the motive.

EX. 8   BACH - Two-Part Invention No. 7

There are several points in Example 8 that merit special mention:

Notice the frequent changes in interval in the various statements of the motive. For example, the interval between the last two notes of the motive is a perfect 5th at the start. In the second measure it becomes an octave, and in later appearances a perfect 4th, a minor and major 6th, a minor 7th, and an augmented 4th. Such changes give fresh interest and allow for different harmonic suggestions.

70

In measures 7 and 8, only the first three notes of each statement of the motive are in contrary motion.

It is usually necessary to depart from a strict statement of thematic material at cadence points.

In measures 7 and 8 there is a dominant pedal point, in G major, in the upper voice, and in measures 15–17 a dominant pedal point, in E minor, in the lower voice. These passages are particularly effective because of the fact that both voices are in motion during most of the invention. The pedal point provides a certain element of repose, and a relief from constant activity in both voices.

The cadences in measures 7, 9, and 13 act as "punctuation" and mark the sections of the invention, the one in measure 9 being perhaps a bit lighter than the others in terms of formal division. Very often the voices exchange material at such cadence points.

Stretto is involved in measures 11 and 12 and provides a climax to the first half of the invention.

Sequences are abundant.

Notes are sometimes added at the beginning of the motive or between consecutive statements of it in order to carry on the rhythmic motion, as at measure 20, bottom voice, and elsewhere.

In analyzing inventions, some of the points to be noted are these:

1) Characteristics of the motive
    Length
    Start on tonic note or elsewhere
    Harmonies implied
    Position in measure, on the beat or after rest, etc.
    Striking melodic or rhythmic features
    Whether announced alone or with accompanying voice
    If accompanied, whether added voice is free material or a counter-motive used later
2) The imitation
    At the octave?
    Exactly like first announcement or changed?
    Nature of other voice, counter-motive or free?
3) Subsequent announcements
    Keys involved and their relationship to home key
    Motive complete or only partially stated?
4) Episodes
    Source of material
    Length
    Modulations effected

71

5) Rhythmic relationship between voices; use of ties or rests
6) Sections
   Use of cadences
   Exchange of voices between one section and another
   Use of same or different harmonic succession
   Relative proportions of sections; symmetry or lack of it

SUGGESTED ASSIGNMENTS

Page in
Workbook

1. *Analyze one or more of the Bach Two-Part Inventions as specified by the instructor.*

2. *Write counter-motives to the invention motives given in the Workbook.*   33

3. *Using one of the motives in the Workbook, write the beginning of a two-part invention. This is to include at least two announcements of the motive in the tonic and two in the dominant (as much as is shown in the chart on page 61 in this chapter).*

4. *Complete the invention begun for 3.*

5. *Write five motives suitable for use in a two-part invention. Have some in major and some in minor; use different tempos and different meter signatures.*

6. *Using one of the motives written for 5, write the beginning of a two-part invention; first four announcements as specified in 3, above.*

7. *Complete the invention begun for 6.*

¶ Three = Voice

Counterpoint

7

Writers on counterpoint have frequently extolled the virtues of three-voice texture. They stress the fact that it allows for greater harmonic completeness and richness than does two-voice counterpoint, yet still maintains clarity of individual line. Also, they point out that much of the world's finest music is based on a three-voice fabric. The most obvious examples are trio-sonatas from the Baroque period, but a great deal of other music, if reduced to its skeletal form, would prove to consist of only three basic voices.

Our first work in three-part counterpoint will be in 1:1 form—that is, with all three voices moving in the same time values. The presence of a third voice gives us the ability to sound all three notes of a triad at once, whereas in two part writing we were forced to suggest the harmony with only two notes sounded vertically. However, there are times when, usually for linear reasons, two of the voices will take the same chord tone, either in unison or an octave or two octaves apart. There is then a choice as to which of the remaining two chord members to include and which to omit. In our work in two-part counterpoint we discovered that the third of the chord was necessary to define its color quality, and that the root must normally be present for purposes of identification. Therefore the fifth was the chord member best omitted where an omission was necessary. As a rule, the same is true in three-voice counterpoint.

Following are some examples to illustrate usable three-note combinations, and also some to be avoided.

EX. 1

a) Less frequent. See comments in text.

(tripled 5th)

The tripled root should occur only at the beginning or end of exercises. Combinations marked *a* contain either a doubled third or a doubled fifth, and are normally avoided. But there are times when the satisfactory motion of individual voices makes them desirable. Illustrations of such cases follow.

EX. 2

doubled 3rd   doubled 3rd   doubled 5th

Notice that whereas in two-part counterpoint the perfect 4th was too harsh and incomplete to be used as an essential interval, it becomes usable in three-voice writing because the third voice can complete the triad, as at the beginning of Example 2.

In seventh chords, one note must always be omitted, since it is obviously impossible to sound four notes with only three voices (see Example 3).

EX. 3

a) Less frequent; doubtful because of missing third.
b) Chords so marked are forms of the incomplete V7 (VII triad).

74

Most of the usable patterns demonstrated with the V⁷ in Example 3 can also be used on other scale steps to give secondary seventh chords, with the exception of the chords marked *b*. These would merely sound like triads on other scale steps, since they would not contain the tritone that suggests the dominant seventh chord.

The incomplete V⁹ (or the VII⁷, using the other terminology) does not occur frequently in this style, but is sometimes useful. Examples of it along with the resolutions are shown next.

EX. 4

Parallel 5ths are still to be avoided in general, but there is one special case in which the effect of going from a diminished 5th to a perfect 5th in the two top voices of three-voice counterpoint is acceptable (Example 5*a*). These 5ths must not be used in *outer* voices, however (Example 5*b*).

EX. 5

The principle involved here is that the ear hears the outer voices in three-part counterpoint as being slightly more important than the inner voice. The fact that the outer voices in Example 5*a* move in parallel 10ths seems to take the stigma off the 5ths, while in the *b* version the 5ths are conspicuous because of their position as outer voices.

Partly because of the somewhat less prominent character of the middle voice, and partly because it is extremely difficult to write a middle voice which involves no consecutive repetition, the prohibition against repeated notes in 1:1 is relaxed with respect to the middle voice only. Even there, repeated notes should be employed only where a change of note is awkward or im-

75

possible, and every effort should be made to create as interesting and strong a middle voice as possible.

Remember that, just as in two-part writing, the harmonies implied by the voices must be considered. This point was discussed in Chapter 3, pages 22 to 24. Remember, too, that the melodic form of the minor scale is the one normally used. (Chapter 2, page 10)

In the exercises to follow, the middle voice may be put on the upper or lower staff, depending on which pitch notation is the more convenient. If desired, three separate staves may be employed, and in that case the middle voice may be written in one of the C clefs.

The three voices should be kept within the following range limits.

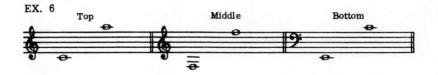

EX. 6

The rules of spacing which are applied in four-voice harmony are relaxed somewhat here; that is, it is sometimes necessary to have more than an octave between the upper voices, though such arrangements should not continue for long.

In these exercises, remember that the results should not be mere successions of three-part harmonies, but three individual lines with independent curves. Each added voice should be sung or played separately in order to test its ability to stand alone as a good melodic line. To achieve this end with the middle voice will probably be more difficult than with the other two.

Example 7 illustrates the sort of exercise that will be assigned next. One voice is given and the other two are to be added in 1:1 fashion. In Example 7 the given line was specified as the bottom voice, and the upper two voices have been added.

EX. 7

CHROMATIC ALTERATION

Three-voice counterpoint lends itself more easily to chromatic alteration than does two-voice counterpoint, because the harmony can be defined more explicitly with three notes. The following partial list of altered chords in major with resolutions may serve to illustrate chromatic possibilities of a harmonic nature in three-voice writing. The chords are grouped according to the scale step altered, first those in which the altered tonic appears, and so on. Chords that contain two alterations are grouped on the basis of their lowest alteration.

EX. 8

Notice that in many of these progressions the altered chord has the function of "secondary dominant" or dominant embellishing chord of the diatonic chord that follows it.

Sometimes an implication of chromatic harmony results from the fact that a line being counterpointed is in itself chromatic. This is true in the next example, where the top line is a fugue subject, extended.

EX. 9   BACH - W. T. C., Vol. II,   Fugue 6

At other times, for the sake of added richness and interest, chromatic alterations are introduced in counterpointing a predominantly diatonic line, as in Example 10.

EX. 10   BACH - Durch Adam's Fall ist ganz verderbt (Organ)

It should perhaps be pointed out that a concentrated use of altered chords, contrapuntally implied, in the style we are imitating is rare. A constant reliance on them would be in questionable taste, and even more monotonous than a consistently diatonic treatment.

The following, though not all examples of *three*-part writing, are especially good as illustrations of Bach's approach to chromatic materials, and are recommended for study: *Two-Part Invention No. 11; Three-Part Invention No. 9; The Well Tempered Clavier*—Vol. I, Fugues 12 and 24— Vol. II, Fugues 6 and 22, Prelude 20.

CHROMATIC MODULATION

In Examples 9 and 10 no actual modulation was involved. The chromatic harmonies served mainly as dominant embellishments of diatonic harmonies. However, modulation can be effected very easily by chromatic means, as illustrated in Example 11. This example is presented not as true counterpoint but merely as a 1:1 version showing the harmonic framework that might serve as the basis for a contrapuntal passage.

EX. 11

Pivotal (common-note) modulations such as those shown in Example 12 necessarily involve chromatic alterations.

EX. 12

This mention of chromatic modulation was prompted by the discussion of chromatic alteration in general, and should not be taken as a suggestion that the device is especially characteristic of the eighteenth-century idiom. Although it does occur in that style, it is little used as compared with the common-chord type of modulation, and it is far more characteristic of nineteenth-century music, particularly that of Franck and Wagner.

SUSPENSIONS

Suspensions in two-voice counterpoint were discussed earlier. The basic process is the same in three-voice writing; a note belonging to one harmony is retained, either by a tie or by repetition, during the next harmony, to which it is dissonant and into which it normally resolves. Example 13 shows an excerpt that abounds in suspensions. In some of them a half note beginning on the second beat takes the place of two tied quarter notes.

EX. 13   BACH - W. T. C., Vol. I, Prelude 24

It might be well to examine the effect of various suspensions. The following are all satisfactory.

EX. 14

Suspensions into the third of the chord (*a, b,* and *c*) and into the root (*d* and *e*) are stronger than those that resolve to the fifth of the chord (*f*). Since the charm of suspensions lies in the dissonant element they create, those containing a 2nd or a 7th are somewhat more effective than the others. The dissonance is of course most acute when a *minor* 2nd is involved, as in *e*.

In three-voice writing, suspensions are described in terms of the intervals between the *bass* and the suspended voice (or, if the suspension is in the bass, in terms of the intervals between the outer voices).

In *g* and *h* the suspension is prepared on the second half of the preceding beat. This arrangement is sometimes useful as a means of introducing suspensions where none of the notes *on* the beat can be retained and resolved downwards into the next harmony, so as to form a suspension.

A possibility we have not used before is demonstrated in *i* and *j*, Example 14. As the resolution of the suspension takes place, one or more members of the chord of resolution move to other chord tones. In *i* the bottom

81

voice moves to the third from the root and in *j* both the top and bottom voices move. A similar device is shown in *k* and *l* where one or more voices move at the point of resolution, but to a *new* harmony instead of the one into which the suspension would normally resolve. Obviously, the note of resolution must fit into the new harmony in such cases.

Certain suspensions that require special comment are shown in Example 15.

EX. 15

When a suspension resolves to the third of a chord, it is generally best not to have that third in another voice at the point of resolution (Example 15*a*). However, when the chord of resolution is a secondary triad and might therefore contain a doubled third, as in *b*, this arrangement is possible.

The suspension into the third of the IV chord involves an objectionable tritone if the fifth of the chord is missing (*c*). Otherwise, this suspension is possible (*d*).

Remember that in suspensions involving more than one beat the suspended note must fall on a strong beat; suspensions that resolve within a beat may occur on any beat.

The "chain" suspension, mentioned earlier, is demonstrated in Example 16.

EX. 16   BACH - W. T. C., Vol. I, Fugue 8

The bass in chain suspensions frequently moves alternately down a 4th and up a 2nd.

EX. 17

It is possible to suspend more than one note at a time.   Example 18 contains a number of double suspensions.

EX. 18   BACH - W. T. C., Vol. II, Prelude 12

Double retardations are also possible.

Delayed resolutions of suspensions occur very often in Bach's music. Example 19 illustrates this arrangement on the first beat of each measure. The basic harmonic progression has been added below the excerpt in order to show the suspensions more clearly.

EX. 19   BACH - W. T. C., Vol. I, Fugue 12

This last example also illustrates, at *a* and *b,* the use of a harmonic change at the point of resolution.   At *a* we would expect F minor, at *b,* D-flat major.

As mentioned in an earlier chapter, contrapuntal music sometimes makes use of an arpeggiated harmonic succession that includes a suspension. Example 20 gives a further illustration of this device.

EX. 20   BACH - W. T. C., Vol. I, Fugue 7

CONVERSION OF 1:1 TO OTHER RHYTHMS

Our next project will consist of converting 1:1 counterpoint in three voices to versions involving 2:1, 3:1, and 4:1 rhythms, with the motion distributed among the voices. (Example 19 on page 83 is a good illustration of counterpoint in which the motion is more or less evenly distributed among the voices.)   As in similar exercises done earlier with two voices, this will be accomplished by adding notes such as chord tones, passing tones, suspensions and auxiliaries to the basic 1:1 version.   Example 21 shows a short 1:1 counterpoint which serves as the basis for the converted versions that follow it.

EX. 21

*An occasional passing seventh may be used even in the 1:1 versions.

Example 22, below, illustrates what this might look like when converted to a 2:1 rhythm.

EX. 22

Examples 23a and b show possible 3:1 and 4:1 versions respectively.

EX. 23

a

b

85

Obviously, these results have more the character of figurated harmony than of real counterpoint. This process, a somewhat mechanical one, is introduced here chiefly as a stepping stone between 1:1 counterpoint and the free three-voice counterpoint that is to follow. Of course, even in writing free counterpoint directly, the 1:1 basis must be considered, though not as methodically or consciously as in these exercises.

THE ADDITION OF TWO VOICES TO A GIVEN MELODY

The last exercise to be assigned in connection with this chapter consists of adding two voices in free counterpoint to a given chorale melody. The two added voices may both take the same type of material, or differ in content. In his chorale preludes, Bach very frequently derives his accompanying material from the first phrase of the chorale. This effective device is recommended to the student. In any case, the use of a characteristic figure or pattern will help to give unity and coherence to the music. Examples 4, 5, 6, and 7 in Chapter 10, pages 127 and 128, illustrate some possibilities in contrapuntal accompaniments to chorale melodies. Although they make use of four voices, the general techniques they demonstrate can be applied just as well in three-voice writing.

SUGGESTED ASSIGNMENTS

¶ The Three =
Part Invention

8

The spirit, proportions, and general technique of the three-part invention do not differ essentially from those of the two-part invention. There are, however, certain technical differences, mostly in the initial announcements of the motive, that must be considered.

First of all, at the outset the motive is far more likely to be accompanied by another voice. All the Bach three-part inventions have such an accompanying voice. Most often it consists of free material without much linear importance, which does not appear again. In other cases, it has the status of a counter-motive, and is brought back again along with the motive in some of the succeeding announcements.

The most important difference is that the second announcement of the motive is normally in the *dominant* key rather than the tonic. The third statement then reverts to the tonic key. Since a return to the tonic cannot always be made smoothly within the measures allotted to the motive, there is sometimes a short link passage between the second and third announcements. Such passages are often sequential extensions of the preceding material and may be as short as a few beats or as long as several measures, depending on how long it takes to return gracefully to the tonic key. The most usual plan for the beginning of a three-part invention is shown in Example 1.

Some of the Bach three-part inventions make use of a real counter-motive along with the second announcement of the motive, whereas in others there

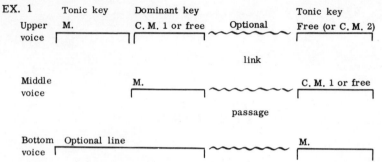

EX. 1

is simply free material at that point. The use of an actual *second* counter-motive is extremely rare, because to be so considered, a melodic element would have to recur repeatedly along with the motive in later portions of the invention. In any case, Bach is highly economical with material and nearly always corroborates any *prominent* or distinctive element by repeating it somewhere in the invention.

A convenient system for referring to the voices is to number them from the top down. Using that system, the order in which the voices announce the motive in Example 1 is 1 2 3. All but two of the Bach three-part inventions follow that plan. However, other orders are quite possible:

3 2 1   2 1 3   2 3 1

The following orders are generally avoided:

3 1 2   1 3 2

For the most part, the motives in the Bach three-part inventions are one to two measures in length. The motive in Example 2, though four measures long, is relatively short in terms of sound.

The beginning of the invention seen in Example 2 conforms to the plan given in Example 1. The added voice is present at the beginning, as well as a four-measure link between the second and third announcements of the motive. An actual counter-motive is used.

In a good many cases, the motives of three-part inventions are constructed like the one in Example 2, in that they end with a group of running notes that do not seem to be part of the motive itself. Rather they appear to be notes added on for the purpose of maintaining the rhythmic flow, and to lead smoothly to the first note of the counter-motive, or whatever material follows. Such notes are sometimes called "intermediate tones," or the group of them may be referred to as a "codetta" or a "melodic link." The latter term is the one that we shall use. When such a series of tones appears consistently at the end of the motive, it is more properly considered part of the motive. It is true that in Example 2 the running sixteenths appear at the end of the motive each time it is announced, but in later portions of the

88

EX. 2   BACH - Three-Part Invention No. 13

invention they do not. Consequently we come to feel that they are not an integral part of the motive.

The invention cited in Example 3 differs from the one we have just discussed in that it involves no counter-motive. Also, there is no adding of measures to form a link passage between the second and third announcements. However, there is a melodic link between the motive and the

89

material that follows. The first time, in measure 2, the link leads to the dominant key, but at the end of the second announcement, in measure 4, it is changed by the use of contrary motion so as to effect the necessary modulation back to the tonic.

EX. 3   BACH – Three–Part Invention No. 12

Example 4 illustrates a particular arrangement which needs a word of explanation. In the third measure, the second statement of the motive begins on the dominant note, but the *harmony* implied on the first beat is the original tonic. The choice of that harmony here rather than the dominant, merely springs from the fact that the motive ends on a note which clearly implies the tonic. A modulation to the dominant key begins on the next beat, and we would still speak of this announcement as being "in the dominant key"—or, of course, simply "at the 5th."

90

EX. 4   BACH - Three-Part Invention No. 10

Three-Part Invention Number 4 follows this same pattern.

TONAL IMITATION

As a first step in exploring the principle of tonal imitation, let us examine the excerpt shown in Example 5.

EX. 5 ·   BACH - Three-Part Invention No. 8

If the top voice in measure two had been an exact or "real" imitation of the motive at the 5th, it would have consisted of the following notes:

EX. 6

But the motive as it appears in the second measure of the invention substitutes an F for a G. When such changes occur, the imitation is known as "tonal." The general principle is this: when the dominant note or another dominant element occurs prominently in the motive, the imitation of that portion is usually changed so as to suggest the original tonic instead of the dominant harmony of the dominant key. The imitation of these notes, therefore, is a perfect 4th above the original instead of a perfect 5th above.* The terms "at the 4th" and "at the 5th" are applied not only to notes that are literally a 4th or a 5th higher, but to notes of the same letter names in higher or lower octaves. For instance, if middle C is the note being imitated, any of the following notes would be an imitation at the 5th.

EX. 7

In Example 5 only one note, the dominant note itself, was changed in the tonal answer. However, it is sometimes necessary to change several notes in order to make a satisfactory melodic line or to preserve certain intervallic relationships within the motive ("subject," in the case of fugue). In the following, for example, the first eleven notes of the motive are imitated tonally. Here, and in other examples to follow, the tonal portion of the imitation is indicated by an X, which is followed by a bracket in the case of a *series* of tonal notes.

EX. 8   BACH - Three-Part Invention No. 1

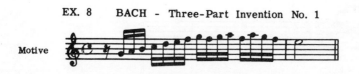

Motive

---

* It has been suggested that tonal imitation arose chiefly because of a desire to avoid the supertonic note of the original key in the imitation. Certainly the wish to prolong the feeling of the tonic key must have been an important factor.

92

Imitation

Real imitation would have been:

No hard and fast rule exists as to when tonal imitation should be employed, but the cases in which it commonly appears can be described in the two statements that follow.

1) Tonal imitation is generally used when the dominant element—usually the dominant note, but occasionally the leading tone—occurs at or near the beginning of the motive. Examples 5 and 8 involve the use of the dominant note at the beginning. In Example 9 the dominant note, F, occurs *near* the beginning, but in the imitation, the notes preceding the B-flat are also changed, to make a smooth line and to preserve the scale-wise character of the motive.

EX. 9   BACH - Three-Part Invention No. 14

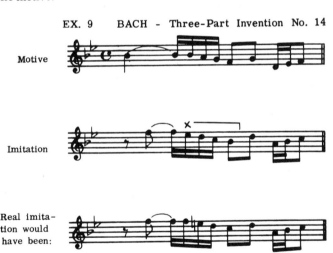

Motive

Imitation

Real imitation would have been:

Example 10 shows a fugue subject in which the second note is the leading tone and the third and fourth beats suggest dominant harmony. In the imitation or "answer," the substituted notes suggest the original tonic harmony.

EX. 10   BACH - W. T. C., Vol. I, Fugue 23

Subject

Answer

Real answer
would have
been:

In Example 11 the motive or fugue subject opens with a leap from the tonic to the dominant note.   When this occurs tonal imitation is almost always involved in the answer.

EX. 11   BACH - W. T. C., Vol. I, Fugue 8

Subject

Answer
(tonal)

Real answer
would have
been:

In such cases the tonic-dominant leap is answered in the imitation by a leap from the dominant note to the tonic note, both of the original key.

2) Tonal imitation is normally used when there is a modulation to the dominant at the end of the motive or subject.   This is illustrated in Example 12.

EX. 12   HANDEL - Concerto Grosso in C.

Subject

Answer

Real answer
would have
been:

It can easily be seen that if some adjustment were not made in the imitation, it would end in the dominant of the dominant, and the return to the tonic key for the third announcement would then be more of a problem. Tonal changes and adjustments such as this are best made at inconspicuous points, so that they will have as little effect as possible on essential features of the melody.

One important exception to these general principles must be mentioned. Tonal imitation is not generally used if the change it involves would do violence to some highly characteristic element of the motive or to a pattern, sequential or otherwise. In the light of what has been said, the fugue subject partially quoted in Example 13 might be expected to call for a tonal answer, since it begins with a leap from tonic to dominant. However, tonal imitation would spoil the sequential pattern and the "line within a line" that we hear on the first beat of each measure.

EX. 13   BACH - Fugue in C Minor (Organ) etc.

Subject

Answer

It should also be mentioned that in some cases tonal imitation occurs only in the initial announcements of an invention or fugue, real answers being used after that.

More will be said about tonal imitation in the chapters on fugue.

EXCEPTIONAL FEATURES

A few deviations from the general pattern set up in Example 1 might be mentioned. In Numbers 2 and 15 of Bach's *Three-Part Inventions* the second announcement of the motive is at the octave instead of at the 5th. In Number 6 the third statement of the motive is in the dominant instead of the tonic. Number 5 is completely atypical in structure. It might best be described as a two-part invention in the two upper voices with a free bass which employs the same pattern throughout to outline the harmonic background. It suggests, incidentally, a style often found in trio-sonatas.

95

ANALYSIS

Example 14 consists of a three-part invention with analytical markings added. The use of tonal imitation in this invention was discussed earlier. Other points which should be noted are:

1) The use of the first three notes of the motive to form a sequential episode in measures 4–5, again in measures 15–17, and 19–20.

2) The effective use of stretto in measures 7–10 and 18–19.

3) The two complete statements of the motive in the tonic key in the last three measures. Such statements give a feeling of completion at the close of inventions.

4) The definite cadences in measure 7 (in C major, the dominant key) and in measure 15 (in D minor, the relative minor). These set off one section from another and prevent a "non-stop" effect which might result from too continuous a motion of the voices without a resolution into a temporary point of rest. Of course, there is also a strong cadence at the end. While this fact may seem too obvious to warrant mention, it needs to be stressed because one of the most frequent weaknesses in student counterpoint is the failure to make the final cadence strong enough and stylistically convincing.

EX. 14   BACH - Three-Part Invention No. 8

Episode on begin. of M.

SUGGESTED ASSIGNMENTS

Page in
Workbook

1. *Analyze one or more of Bach's* Three-Part Inventions *as specified by the instructor.*

2. *Write counter-motives to the invention motives given in the* Workbook.   51

3. *Using one of the motives in the* Workbook, *write the beginning of a three-part invention.   This is to include at least as much as is shown in Example 1 on page 88.*

4. *Complete the invention begun for 3.*

5. *Write five motives suitable for use in a three-part invention.   Have some in major and some in minor and use different tempos and meter signatures.*

6. *Using one of the motives written for 5, write the beginning of a three-part invention, through the first four announcements as shown in Example 1 on page 88.*

7. *Complete the invention begun for 6.*

¶ The Canon

9

If a melodic line is duplicated by a second voice which begins later than the first voice, the result is called a canon. One type of canon, the "round," is familiar even to non-musicians through such favorites as *Three Blind Mice* and *Row, Row, Row Your Boat*. Other types have been used in more serious music for centuries. As a rule, the canonic treatment is applied merely to a portion of a work rather than to the entire composition, though such exceptions as the canons in Bach's *The Art of Fugue* could be cited.

The first voice in a canon is known as the "leader," while the imitating voice is called the "follower." If more than two voices are involved, the terms "first follower," "second follower," and so on, are used.

THE TWO-VOICE CANON

The time interval between the entrances of the voices in a canon may be anything from one note to many measures, though the use of either extreme is rare. Example 1 involves a time interval that may be considered about average. It allows enough of the leader to be heard alone first so that the imitation in the follower is apparent to the ear, yet it is not so long that the listener may have difficulty in retaining the beginning of the leader in his mind until the same material appears in the follower.

EX. 1   SCHUMANN - Papillons, No. 3

The canon in Example 2 employs an extremely short time interval. The imitation in this case is particularly hard to hear because the voices are placed in different metric positions, the first beginning on an anacrusis and the second on a beat.

EX. 2   MOZART - Sonata, K. 576

In addition to the time interval, another variable in canonic writing is the harmonic interval between the voices—that is, the distance measured vertically between the first note of the leader and that of the follower. The harmonic interval employed in Examples 1 and 2 was the octave, which is likely to work out most naturally and easily in maintaining unity of key. On the other hand, it involves a certain problem of harmonic variety, a point that will be further elaborated at the end of the chapter.

Two-voice canons at the unison are rare, especially unaccompanied. In Example 3 the second upper voice reproduces the first at the unison; the free voice at the bottom does not take part in the canon, but provides harmonic definition and rhythmic flow.

EX. 3   BACH - Goldberg Variations (Var. 3)

In canons at the unison, crossing of the voices is inevitable, and it is likely to occur also in canons at such smaller intervals as the 2nd and 3rd.

The 4th, 5th, and 6th all figure frequently as harmonic intervals in canonic writing. The 7th is also used, but more rarely. In Example 4 a canon at the 5th below from a Bach organ work is shown. The pedal note in the last measure of the example is the beginning of the chorale melody, to which the canon forms an accompaniment.

EX. 4   BACH - Canonic Variations on Vom Himmel hoch (Var. 2)

In canons at intervals other than the octave or unison, it is usually necessary to change the inflections (sharps, flats, or absence of these) of certain notes in the follower to achieve unity of tonality. Sometimes even in canons at the unison or the octave such changes are introduced to imply desired harmonic progressions. The F-sharp and G-sharp in the last measure of Example 4 illustrate this use. In any case, the canon is still considered "strict" as long as the basic pitches, apart from accidentals, conform to the canonic pattern.

The endings of canons are often free, in order to allow for a satisfactory cadence.

101

Canons at the 9th and 10th are somewhat easier to write than those at the 2nd and 3rd because crossing of the voices is not so likely to be present. The 9th is the harmonic interval in Example 5.

EX. 5   BACH - Goldberg Variations (Var. 27)

The 12th is not uncommon as a harmonic interval, but the 11th is seldom encountered.   Harmonic intervals of more than a 12th are rare.

The use of diminished and augmented harmonic intervals in the style we are considering is out of the question because of the difficulties involved in preserving unity of key and reasonable chordal implications.

Whether a melody can be treated canonically (and if so, what interval will be successful) is determined by the nature of the melody itself.   Many melodies do not lend themselves at all to canonic treatment, while others may make effective canons at several different intervals.   In any case, a certain amount of trial and rejection is usually required before successful results are achieved.   Occasionally, however, a composer may arrive at a happy canonic arrangement by chance.

An excellent work for study in connection with canons is Bach's *Goldberg Variations*, excerpts from which have already been quoted here.   In that monumental set of thirty variations, Variation 3 and those whose numbers are multiples of three are canons, each at a different interval.   Moreover, the interval in each case is the number of the variation divided by three.   For example, in Variation 9 the canon is at the 3rd.

CANONS USING THREE OR MORE VOICES

When three or more voices are combined in canonic fashion, the time interval and the harmonic interval used between the first two voices may or may not be used again for the succeeding voices. In the three-voice canon shown in Example 6, both the harmonic interval (an octave) and the time interval (one measure) are the same. Incidentally, these voices then become an accompaniment to another canon in longer values, which begins in the fourth measure on the middle staff.

EX. 6   BACH - Christe, Du Lamm Gottes

Example 7, a stretto from a fugue, has the basic structure of a four-voice canon, although the imitation is not carried out strictly. Notice that three different time intervals and two harmonic intervals are involved here.

EX. 7   BACH - W. T. C., Vol. I, Fugue 1

In the four-voice canon shown in Example 8, the time interval is the same in each case, while the harmonic interval is not. However, the alto and soprano entrances are the same distance apart as those in the bass and tenor voices.

EX. 8   ALBRECHTSBERGER - Four-Voice Canon

Example 23 on page 114 might be cited as an illustration of a four-voice canon that uses the same time interval (two beats) and the same harmonic interval (a 5th) between all the entrances.

Canons in more than four voices are relatively rare. Example 9 shows a final stretto from a fugue, an impressive example of five-voice canonic writing. The use of a descending 5th rather than a 4th at the beginning of the answers (the second and fourth announcements of the fugue subject here) is of course an application of the principle of tonal imitation discussed in Chapter 8. An extra staff has been added here so that the movement of individual voices can be seen more clearly than in the usual notation on two staves.

EX. 9   BACH - Fugue No. 22 from W. T. C., Vol. I

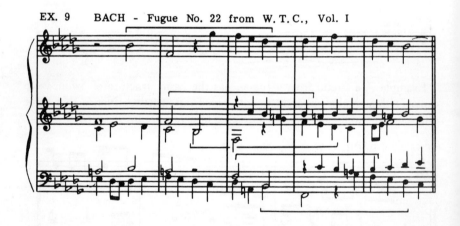

CANONS USING SPECIAL DEVICES

The devices of contrary motion (inversion), augmentation, diminution, and retrograde motion that were mentioned in the discussion of inventions may be applied in canonic writing.

Contrary Motion

In Example 10 the middle voice imitates the upper by contrary motion at the 6th below. The bottom voice is free and does not take part in the canon.

EX. 10   BACH - Canonic Variations on Vom Himmel hoch (Var. 5)

The chart in Example 11 shows what happens to the various scale steps when they are imitated in contrary motion in a canon at the unison or octave.

EX. 11

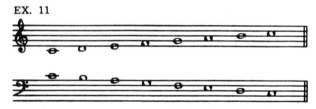

The note D in the leader will be answered by B in the follower, A by E, and so on. Notice that the dominant note in the leader is answered by the subdominant note in the follower, and the subdominant note by the dominant note. Similar charts could be made to show what notes result when the the voices begin at intervals other than the octave or unison, and proceed by contrary motion. Remember that the notes seen in the same line vertically in such charts will not actually sound together in a canon using contrary motion, since the voices do not start at the same time. If they did—that is, if the time interval were reduced to nothing—the result would be called a "mirror" * rather than a canon in contrary motion.

* The term "mirror" has also been applied to the crab canon, which will soon be discussed, the mirroring in that case being horizontal rather than vertical.

Augmentation

In Example 12 the two outer voices form a canon at the octave with the bottom voice moving in values twice as long as those in the leader. The middle voice is free, but imitates the upper one at the start.

EX. 12   BACH - Canonic Variations on Vom Himmel hoch (Var. 4)

In Example 13 the middle voice imitates the top voice in augmentation. The singers' words have been omitted here.

EX. 13   BRAHMS - Requiem (Part 5)

Example 14 is a stretto from a fugue. The top voice is an augmentation of the bottom one, while the middle voice is augmented in part and con-

106

tains some changes in the relative value of the notes.

EX. 14   BACH - W.T.C., Vol. I, Fugue 8

A rare case of the combination of augmentation and contrary motion in a canon is seen in the excerpt from *The Art of Fugue* which is shown in Example 15.

EX. 15   BACH - The Art of Fugue (Canon No. 1)

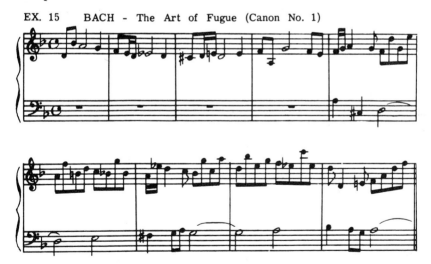

Although these examples use augmentation in which the follower moves twice as slowly as the leader, other time relationships between voices are possible in an augmented version. For instance, if the leader is in 6/8, 9/8, or 12/8, its eighth-notes will normally be answered by dotted quarters in the augmented follower, since quarter-notes would not conform to the natural division of the measure. It is even possible to have a doubly augmented follower, with values four times as long as those in the leader. Notice that when augmentation is involved the follower can never overtake the leader and that, in fact, it gets farther and farther behind, in terms of imitation, as the canon progresses. Bach sometimes solves this problem by stating the leader twice against one augmented statement in the follower.

Diminution

In a canon in diminution, just the opposite process applies. Since the follower is moving in values shorter than those of the leader, it soon overtakes the leader. If the canon is at the octave and is continuous, parallel octaves between the voices are inevitable at that point. This is shown in Example 16.

EX. 16

From then on, the voices reverse their roles. The one that started out as the follower becomes the leader, and the former leader follows in what amounts to augmentation. In actual music, the "overtaking" process just mentioned and the consequent parallel intervals it entails are seldom allowed to happen, especially in a canon at the octave. Sometimes the canonic treatment is abandoned before one voice can overtake the other. In the fugue quoted in Example 17, for instance, the bottom voice finishes the statement of the subject and goes on to other material before the diminished imitation in the middle voice reaches the point where parallel octaves would have occurred.

EX. 17   BACH - The Art of Fugue (Fugue No. 6)

The third voice, which enters in the third measure, illustrates diminution alone, while the second voice, beginning in measure 2, involves contrary motion in addition to diminution.

Another way of avoiding the overtaking process in a canon in diminution is to start both voices at the same time, at what would have been the overtaking point. Although such an arrangement is contrary to our definition of canon in that the voices enter together rather than consecutively, the exception seems warranted here, whereas it did not in the case of the "mirror." This is because the voices are moving at different speeds, the imitative effect thus being consecutive rather than simultaneous.

In Example 18 a phrase of a chorale melody is stated in the top voice, while the lower three voices make several statements of the same phrase in double diminution. The first two of these form a brief canon in themselves. At the end of the example the alto voice overtakes the soprano, but the resulting parallelism is not objectionable because it does not involve octaves or 5ths. Also, when combined with the other voices, it forms a good harmonic progression.

EX. 18   BACH - Dies sind die heil'gen zehn Gebot'

The Canon

Retrograde Motion

In a retrograde canon, also called crab canon or *canon cancrizans,* the melody played backwards accompanies the melody in its original form. As might be expected, this type of canon can easily become a mere mechanical feat in which the difficult requirements of the form are met without contributing anything very satisfying as music. Furthermore, few ears can detect the imitative relationship between voices when they are sounded forward and backward at once, particularly when they start at the same time. Example 19 shows one of the very few crab canons in musical literature. The beginning and end of the original notation are first shown, twelve measures in the middle having been omitted here for reasons of space. Then follows the realization in full.

EX. 19   BACH - Retrograde Canon from "The Musical Offering"

THE PERPETUAL CANON

Canons which lead back to the beginning and therefore allow for as many repetitions as desired are called perpetual canons, infinite canons, eternal canons, or circle canons. Because of their particular construction, they have no true cadential ending, unless one is added or the performers agree in advance to end at some point where the parts coincide on a tonic harmony. Such possible ending points are sometimes marked by a fermata. In certain canons in *The Art of Fugue*, the main body of the canon is perpetual, and may be repeated *ad libitum*, but there is a coda of several measures to provide a satisfactory ending.

The Round

A special type of the perpetual canon is the round, which is normally a

111

vocal form with words. It is generally sung by three or more voices, and each singer or group of singers goes back to the beginning after completing the last phrase. Instead of being written out on several staves so as to show the voices as they will sound together, rounds are usually written as a single line, with figures to show where each singer or group is to begin. In such cases the canon is at the unison as far as notation is concerned. If men as well as women perform the round, the men will of course sing an octave lower, so that in terms of actual sound the canon ceases to be entirely at the unison. Following is an example of a round as it would usually be notated.

EX. 20   BYRD - Round

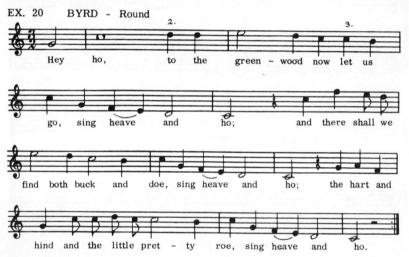

When the first voice or group reaches figure 2, the second voice begins; when the first voice reaches figure 3 and the second voice reaches figure 2, the third voice begins. Example 21 shows the combination of the segments that will result when all three voices are singing.

EX. 21

The plan in three-voice rounds is as follows:

First voice:	a b c ‖: a b c :‖
Second voice:	a b ‖: c a b :‖
Third voice:	a ‖: b c a :‖

(The letters a, b, and c represent the three segments of the melody.)

THE SPIRAL CANON

In the spiral canon, a very rare type, the melody ends in a different key from the one in which it began. There must then be as many repetitions as are necessary to return to the original key, assuming that it is to be reached. For example, in Bach's *Musical Offering* there is a spiral canon which goes from C to D the first time, from D to E the second time, and so on, six playings being needed before the key of C is reached again. Such canons may go around the circle of 5ths or progress by some other interval, as does the one just mentioned.

THE ENIGMA CANON

A type of canon popular long before Bach's day is the "enigma," "puzzle," or "riddle" canon. The notation usually consists of a single melodic line, along with clefs or other clues to indicate the harmonic interval and time interval to be used in working out the actual realization of the canon. Example 22 shows the beginning of such a canon, first in its original notation and then in its realized form. This excerpt is from the *Musical Offering*, which Bach wrote for Frederick the Great, using as a basis a theme composed by the king himself. The canon in the two outer voices forms an accompaniment for an embellished version of the king's theme in the middle voice. The Latin inscription at the beginning says, "May the King's fortunes increase with the growing notes," a reference, of course, to the augmentation involved.

EX. 22   BACH - Canon in Augmentation and Contrary Motion
Original notation from "The Musical Offering"

Thema

Realization

Example 23 shows first the notation and then the realization of the beginning of a four-voice canon in which each voice enters a 5th higher than the preceding voice.

EX. 23   BACH - Canon
Notation

Ple – ni sunt coe – li et ter – – – – ra glo–ri – a   tu – a,

114

Realization

THE ACCOMPANIED CANON

In some of the canons quoted so far there was accompaniment to the extent that a free voice, not involved in the canon, was present. Sometimes a much more elaborate accompaniment, either harmonic or linear, is employed. Undoubtedly the best known of all accompanied canons is the one quoted in Example 24, the last movement of the Franck *Sonata for Violin and Piano*. The accompaniment there is essentially chordal.

EX. 24   FRANCK - Sonata for Violin and Piano

Allegretto poco mosso

Dolce cantabile

In the Schumann excerpt that follows, the accompaniment is a bit more linear.

EX. 25   SCHUMANN - Canonisches Liedchen
Nicht schnell und mit innigen Ausdruck

EX. 26   BRAHMS - Liebeslieder Waltzes (No. 16)

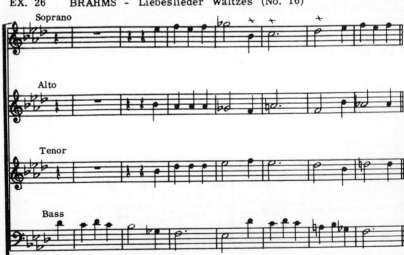

* In a strict inversion these notes would be an octave higher. The use of the lowe[r]
octave is obviously necessary here for reasons of vocal range.

116

In Example 26 the top voice imitates the bottom voice in contrary motion while the middle voices provide harmonic filler. The singers' words are omitted here. Two pianos, whose parts are not indicated, take the canonic lines as well as some harmonic outlines.

THE DOUBLE CANON

The double canon consists of two canons sounded simultaneously. The two leading voices of each canon may start together or consecutively. One canon may be subservient to the other and have the quality of an accompaniment, or the two may be of equal importance. In Example 27 the canon on the chorale melody seems to be somewhat more important than the canon in triplets.

EX. 27   BACH - In Dulci Jubilo (Chorale Prelude for Organ)

In Examples 28 and 29, which show two other possible arrangements in double-canon writing, the voices are approximately equal in importance. The Mozart excerpt is a rare example of a perpetual canon for instruments rather than voices. Additional measures not shown here lead back to the beginning.

EX. 28   MOZART - Double Canon

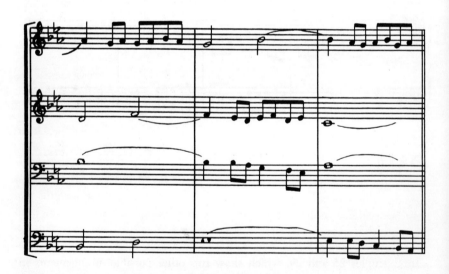

The words to be sung in the Schumann canon that follows have been omitted here.

EX. 29   SCHUMANN - Die Kapelle

CONCERNING THE WRITING OF CANONS

Although the writing of each type of canon involves particular problems, some of which will be mentioned shortly, there is one general suggestion that can be given.   Instead of composing the entire leader and then attempting to make it form a canon with itself, begin by writing the leader only up to the point where the follower is to enter.   This same material can then be written in the follower at whatever harmonic interval is being used and the leader continued in a manner consistent with good counterpoint. This material in the leader will in turn be transferred to the follower, and so on.   As an illustration of this procedure, the segments of the canon in Ex. 30 have been bracketed to show the order in which they were written down.   Of course a good deal of trial and rejection was involved in arriving at this final version.

As intimated earlier, the chief problem in writing canons at the octave or unison is that of avoiding harmonic monotony. The problem arises because the notes of segment 1 in the leader are repeated as segment 2 in the follower. Segment 3, which is a counterpoint for segment 2, is then repeated as segment 4 in the follower, and so on. Consequently, if the notes are always given the same harmonic implication, the canon is likely to reiterate the same harmony indefinitely. The solution is obviously to change the harmonic implications of certain notes where that seems indicated for the sake of variety. In C major, for example, the note G could be the fifth of the tonic chord, the root of the dominant, the third of the mediant, or the seventh of a submediant seventh chord. It could even be made to sound nonharmonic.

In writing a canon in contrary motion it is generally helpful to make out a chart similar to the one in Example 11, using the particular harmonic interval involved in the canon, to show the result of inverting the various notes.

In a canon in augmentation, avoid very long values or continued suggestions of the same harmony in the leader. If this is not done, the augmented imitation will tend to bog down rhythmically or harmonically.

The opposite is true of canons in diminution. If the leader contains very short values, the diminution in the follower is likely to sound unnaturally hurried, somewhat like a record being played at too fast a speed. Similarly, the implied harmonic changes must not succeed each other too swiftly in the leader, or the result will be unmusical and bewildering when the voice is played twice as fast in the follower.

120

The procedure for writing a canon in retrograde motion is to compose the first half of the leader, then write that part backwards as the last half of the follower. Next, by a process of trial and error, find a line that will work forward as the last half of the leader, and backward as the first half of the follower.

In writing a round canon, notate the segments of the canon one above the other, so that their combined effect can be easily seen. Assuming that the round is for voices, be sure to keep it within a practical range. From

is a range suitable for all types of voices, the men's voices sounding an octave lower, of course.

Finally, remember that the test of these canonic arrangements is how they sound, not how impressive they may look on paper. Also, they must not be considered ends in themselves, but rather devices for adding musical interest at points where they fit in naturally.

SUGGESTED ASSIGNMENTS

1. Write examples of the following canons as specified by the instructor:

  two-voice: at the octave
    at another interval
    in contrary motion
    in augmentation
    in diminution
    in retrograde motion
  three-voice: at any intervals desired
    a round (use of words optional)
  four-voice: at any intervals
    a double canon
  accompanied

2. Bring in two examples of canon at the octave and two examples of canon at other intervals.

¶ Forms Based

on the Chorale

10

Ever since Luther's day, the chorale * has been the chief
basis of Protestant church music. Chorale melodies were, in many cases,
secular folk songs adapted for church use by the addition of sacred words,
the latter often being translations into German of Latin texts used in the
Catholic service. Bach carried on not only the tradition of chorale harmonization dating back to the sixteenth century, but also the baroque practices
begun by Scheidt and Schein of incorporating the chorale tunes in pieces
written in true organ style.

Among Bach's large and impressive body of works based on the chorale
are chorale preludes, variations, chorale fantasias, fugues, and fughettas, all
for the organ. Nearly all his motets make use of a chorale at some point,
often at the end; and in the cantatas the chorale likewise figures importantly.
Of course many other composers, including some living today, have written
in these forms. However, Bach's works are so rich and so varied that they
represent the crowning achievement in this realm of music, and it is therefore natural to quote principally from them.

For the benefit of readers who may not be familiar with the organ and
the notation for it, a few comments on the instrument may be helpful.
The notes to be played on the "manuals" or keyboards are written on the

---

* This spelling seems preferable to "choral" (the German spelling which is sometimes used in English) because it avoids possible confusion with the adjective "choral,"
meaning sung by a chorus.

upper two staves, while the part to be played by the feet is written on the bottom staff. The written range of the pedals is ⨎⨎⨎⨎⨎ . An eight-foot stop on the organ produces the same pitch as the written note, a four-foot stop a pitch an octave higher, and a sixteen-foot stop a pitch an octave lower. Indications for one or the other of these are occasionally given by Bach, but otherwise no registration (choice of stops) is specified in his organ music, or in other organ music of that period.

THE CHORALE PRELUDE

The chorale prelude originated as an organ composition designed to be performed during the church service before or after the singing of the chorale by the congregation, or between stanzas. The term as used today does not necessarily imply this actual use in a religious service, and is applied in a more general sense to works that elaborate on a chorale. However, it is usually understood to exclude straightforward harmonizations of chorale melodies, such as might be used to accompany the actual singing of the chorale. The majority of Bach's chorale preludes have four voices; a few use three, five, or six voices, while the use of only two is extremely rare.

The principal elements to be mentioned in connection with chorale preludes are these:

a) The chorale melody, or C. F. for *cantus firmus*. In their original form, *cantus firmi* were written in long note values, chiefly half-notes or longer, and they often retain this characteristic in chorale preludes. On the other hand, the *fermata* (⌒), which was used to mark the last note of each phrase in the original form of the chorale melodies,* is less often seen in chorale preludes and other chorale forms.

b) Motivic material derived from the C. F., most often from the beginning, but involving shorter time values and much greater rhythmic interest and variety than the original melody.

c) Other material, not derived from the C. F., which accompanies either or both of the above (a and b).

There are, unfortunately, no generally accepted names for the various types of chorale prelude. They are listed below by means of brief descriptive phrases.

---

* The view most widely held today is that the *fermata* as used in chorale melodies was not intended to indicate an actual hold.

1) Embellished harmonization
2) Ornamented C. F.
3) Motivic accompaniment of C. F.
4) Canonic treatment
5) Material derived from C. F., but C. F. itself not present
6) Phrases of C. F. superimposed periodically on motivic composition
7) Ritornelle construction—initial material returns periodically between phrases of C. F.

Let us consider each of these types in turn:

Type 1: The chorale melody is harmonized in four voices which are embellished rather plentifully with passing tones, suspensions, or other non-harmonic or harmonic tones. As a rule, the C. F. receives less embellishment than the other voices, and is likely to be presented with only occasional departures from its original form. This type of chorale prelude is obviously not far removed from a basic unadorned harmonization. In the example that follows, the original chorale melody is shown above the excerpt for purposes of comparison.

EX. 1

C. F.

BACH - Herzlich thut mich verlangen (Vol. V*, No. 27)

Man.

Ped.

---

* Here and elsewhere in this chapter, the volume numbers cited in connection with Bach's organ works are those of the Peters Edition.

Type 2: The chorale melody, usually in the top voice, is ornamented, often quite elaborately, while the other parts remain relatively simple.   Sometimes the notes of the original C. F. are shifted in the process of ornamentation. The objective here is obviously to convert the C. F. into a more florid and plastic line.   This kind of chorale prelude shows the influence of elaboration in vocal music.

In the next example the ornamentation of the C. F. is far less florid. In fact, the simplicity of the rhythmic pattern here is more characteristic of Type 1, and the example could even be considered a kind of bridge between that species and the more ornate arrangements characteristic of Type 2.   Nevertheless, it seems to belong under this heading because the chief emphasis in it is on the decoration of the C. F., accomplished in this

EX. 2

C. F.

BACH - Wenn wir in höchsten Nöthen sein (Vol. V, No. 51)

Man.

Ped.

case mainly by the use of non-harmonic tones. These often occur *on* the beat here and then resolve to the notes of the C. F., so that the original chorale melody is somewhat hidden or disguised.

Later in this chorale prelude, phrases of the embellished C. F. are presented in inner voices rather than in the soprano.

EX. 3

BRAHMS - Es ist ein Ros' entsprungen (No. 8 of Eleven Chorale Preludes)

Type 3: The C. F. is stated, usually in the top voice, in more or less its original form, without extended breaks between phrases. It may be accompanied by motivic material in all the other voices. Example 4 illustrates this arrangement as well as the derivation of the recurrent motive from the beginning of the C. F.

126

EX. 4   BACH - Christ ist erstanden (Vol. V, No. 4)

Or the pedals may take independent material not derived from the C. F. (Example 5).
Such an arrangement is likely to be used when the motivic material played on the manuals does not lend itself to performance on the pedals; or it may be introduced for purely musical reasons. Often independent pedal parts involve a characteristic figure which appears repeatedly on different scale degrees, such as the descending octave leap here in Example 5. Once again, the initial motive in this case is derived from the first three notes of the chorale melody.

EX. 5   BACH - Ach wie nichtig, ach wie flüchtig (Vol. V, No. 1)

A third, though infrequent, possibility under Type 3 is that the voices which accompany the C. F. may all be different from each other, as in Example 6.
In this excerpt, there is no clear-cut derivation of motivic material from the C. F. as in the preceding examples, though there are occasional hints of the C. F. in the other voices.

127

EX. 6   BACH - Da Jesus an dem Kreuze stund (Vol. V, No. 9)

Type 4: The C. F. or the motivic material, or both, are treated canonically. In the following example the chorale melody appears in canon at the 15th in the outer voices, while the two inner voices have a rather free canonic treatment of other material.

EX. 7   BACH - Christus, der uns selig macht (Vol. V, No. 8)

Two examples given in Chapter 9 on canon make use of chorale melodies and should be re-examined at this point. Example 18 on page 109 shows a chorale melody accompanied by the beginning of the same melody in diminution. Example 27 on page 117, is a double canon.

Type 5: The C. F. in its original form does not appear; but the motivic material used is derived from some portion of it, usually the first line, or in some cases from several different portions in turn. The approach is generally imitative and sectional (Example 8).

EX. 8

BACH - Christe, aller Welt Trost (Vol. VII, No. 40b)

The chorale forms mentioned so far are likely to be of relatively small proportions, while those that follow are generally of a larger, more pretentious nature. There is, however, no hard and fast dividing line between the two categories.

Type 6a: This type has an opening section, involving imitation in successive entrances, based on motivic material which is usually derived from the C. F. This portion often suggests the beginning of an invention, or even a three voice fugue exposition if the successive keys of the announcements are tonic, dominant, tonic, and if the motivic material is extended. Against a continuation of this motive treatment, the C. F. then appears in longer note values. At the end of the first phrase, the voice carrying the C. F. rests while motivic material similar to that at the start reappears. The second phrase of the C. F. is then introduced, and so on, until the entire chorale melody has been heard. Example 9 illustrates this type.

EX. 9   BACH - Allein Gott in der Höh' sei Ehr' (Vol. VI, No. 4)

Chorale

Incidentally, it is interesting and astonishing to note the number of different motives that Bach derives from this same C. F. in the nine compositions based on it which appear in Volume VI of his organ compositions. The beginnings of six of these motives, including the one used in Example 9, are shown in Example 10, along with the beginning of the C. F. Notice the variety of meter.

EX. 10   Allein Gott in der Höh' sei Ehr' (Vol. VI, Nos. 4-9)

Type 6b: Another species of this sixth type introduces a new motive for each phrase of the chorale, each motive being derived from the phrase that follows. Of course these motives must have enough in common, especially rhythmically, to produce a unified effect when they occur consecutively. The whole is a bit like a number of short inventions, each being heard first alone and then along with a phrase of the C. F. Or, if each motive is announced in fugal fashion, the result becomes the type of chorale fugue known as "chorale motet."

The most characteristic and important features of this form and some of those to follow would not be seen in a brief excerpt, and since space does not allow for lengthy quotations, examples of these forms will merely be cited rather than reproduced here. For that matter, the short examples cited earlier in the chapter give only a very slight idea of the forms they illustrate, and are not intended to take the place of actual study of these and similar works in their original score form.

Examples
Bach, Organ Compositions, Vol. VI, Nos. 1, 23, 32; Vol. VII, Nos. 43, 58.

Type 7: There is an opening section which is likely to be longer than those in Type 6. Furthermore, it is usually not imitative but is more often constructed according to Period design. Sometimes it is a complete Period or a Double Period. The phrases of the C. F. then appear successively against it, and it is re-stated more or less exactly between certain of these phrases and at the end, following the last phrase of the C. F. This form is sometimes referred to as "Ritornelle with Chorale" because the initial material returns consistently.

Examples
Bach, Organ Compositions, Vol. VI, Nos. 2, 3, 7, 30; Vol. VII, No. 57.

USE OF THE CHORALE MELODY IN VARIOUS VOICES

It has already been said that the C. F. is most often placed in the top voice in chorale preludes. But it may appear in any one of the other

131

voices, either throughout the composition or at any desired point, provided, of course, that each phrase is finished by the voice that started it. Sometimes the various phrases of the chorale are given to the respective voices in turn.

In playing chorale preludes on the organ, it is generally desirable to bring out the C. F. a bit in relation to the other voices by using a slightly louder and/or a different registration for that voice. Consequently it is usually best to arrange to have the C. F. on a separate manual or in the pedals. A special device employed by Bach in some of his organ music consists in having the C. F. played by the pedals as a tenor voice, while the bass is played by a hand on one of the manuals. The use of a four-foot stop for the tenor in the pedals is often necessary in order to bring that voice into the right register. This is true of all but one of the examples cited below.

Examples of C. F. as tenor voice in the pedals
Bach, Organ Compositions, Vol. VII, Nos. 38, 56, 59, 63.

CHORALE VARIATIONS * (OR CHORALE PARTITA)

It is impossible to lay down any definite pattern or set of rules for chorale variations. The treatment of the basic chorale in the course of the work will be governed by the composer's taste and imagination. Some of the well known devices that suggest themselves are: figuration of chordal patterns, treatment of segments of the C. F., changes of harmony, and the addition of new counterpoints. Of course any of the arrangements listed under chorale preludes may be used for individual variations. There must be sufficient contrast between variations and a sense of long line and climax through the work as a whole. In the chorale partitas of Bach and earlier composers, the number of variations usually corresponds with the number of stanzas in the chorale, and the mood of individual stanzas is often reflected in the music.

Examples
Bach, Organ Compositions, Vol. V, Variations on *Christ, du bist der Helle Tag;* Variations on *Sei gegrüsset, Jesu gütig;* Canonic Variations on *Vom Himmel hoch da komm ich her* (quoted in Chapter 9, pages 101, 105, and 106).
Brahms, Motet, Op. 74, No. 2.

* This form and those that follow in this chapter are sometimes also classified as types of the chorale prelude, that term frequently being used in a broad sense.

THE CHORALE FANTASIA

As the name implies, the chorale fantasia is extremely free. It is some-times based on only a portion of the C. F. rather than on the whole. Al-though the form is frequently sectional in a general sense, the sections are not so likely to be sharply defined (for example by perfect cadences at the ends) as they are in variation forms.

Examples

Bach, Organ Compositions, Vol. V, No. 34; Vol. VI, Nos. 7, 15, 27; Vol. VII, No. 36.

CHORALE FUGUES AND FUGHETTAS

Bach's works contain many examples of fugues and fughettas (small fugues) in which the subject is derived from a chorale melody. Example 11 shows the beginnings of a fughetta and a fugue, both based on the C. F. at the top of Example 10.

EX. 11   BACH - Fughetta on: Allein Gott in der Höh' sei Ehr'

BACH - Fugue on: Allein Gott in der Höh' sei Ehr'

As already mentioned, it is possible to use each line of the chorale in turn as the basis of a fugal section. The term "chorale motet" * is often applied to such an arrangement, since the form is closer to the plan of the sixteenth-century motet than to that of the characteristic baroque fugue.

Further discussion of forms combining chorale and fugue is being reserved for Chapter 14.

SUGGESTED ASSIGNMENTS

1. *Analyze a number of works based on the chorale, as specified by the instructor.*

All the following are to be written for the organ and are to be based on a chorale melody (a number of these are given in the Workbook, pages 53 and 55).

2. *Write the beginnings (two or three measures each) of five chorale preludes that illustrate the first five types described in this chapter.*

3. *Write a short chorale prelude, plan optional.*

4. *Write a chorale prelude, the plan to be specified by the instructor.*

5. *Write a set of chorale variations.*

6. *Write a chorale fantasia.*

---

* "Chorale motet" and "chorale fugue" are sometimes used synonymously. The author feels that it is better to reserve "chorale motet" for the particular type of composition described here, and to let "chorale fugue" apply to *any* fugue with a chorale basis.

₵ Invertible Counterpoint

11

Two voices are said to be "invertible" when either one can be used as upper or lower voice with good musical results. The term "double counterpoint" has been widely employed as the equivalent of invertible counterpoint, but since it carries another meaning connected with the double fugue, it offers some chance for confusion and will be avoided here. Also, the word "inversion" must be understood as applying to the relative position or level of the voices, and must not be confused with the device of contrary motion, which is often referred to as inversion.

INVERSION AT THE OCTAVE

By all odds the most frequent and natural form of invertible counterpoint is that in which one of the voices is simply transposed up or down one or more octaves so that it becomes the upper voice instead of the lower, or *vice versa.* In Example 1 two voices are shown first in their original relationship. In *b* the lower voice has been transposed up an octave. In *c* the upper voice has been transposed down an octave. Notice that these two versions produce the same relationship between voices, the only difference being that *b* is an octave higher. In *d* the lower voice has been moved up *two* octaves; that is, the inversion is at the 15th.* Still another possi-

---

* Students frequently contend that the interval of two octaves should be called a 16th, since it appears to be twice as large as an octave. The fallacy in that argument is that there is a note in common between the two octaves, so that the total span is only fifteen scale steps.

bility is shown in *e* where the bottom voice has been transposed up an octave, the top voice down an octave. This is also considered inversion at the 15th, the two transpositions in opposite directions being added together to make this figure. More will be said presently about the system of measuring the intervals concerned in invertible counterpoint.

EX. 1

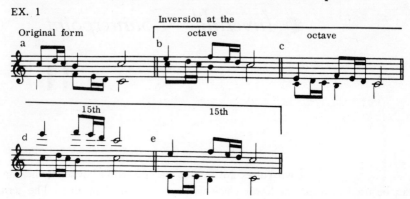

The sort of inversion we have been discussing usually works out more or less automatically. If the original counterpoint is good, the two voices will nearly always sound well when inverted at the octave, or multiples of it. There is only one small difficulty that is likely to arise. If an essential interval of a 5th, generally between the first and fifth scale degrees, appears in the original, the inversion of it will be a 4th. That interval is classed as a dissonance in two-voice counterpoint of this style, and is normally unusable as an essential interval—at least *on* the beat. The obvious conclusion to be drawn here is that the 5th as an essential interval should be avoided in two-voice counterpoint that is to be invertible at the octave. Even in three- or four-voice counterpoint, where the 4th can be used in combination with another triad tone, the fifth scale step itself may prove awkward when put in the lower voice. This is because it often suggests the bass of a tonic chord in second inversion (I_4^6) and the I_4^6 may be used successfully only under certain conditions.

Example 2 gives excerpts from musical literature that illustrate inversion at multiples of the octave.

EX. 2   BACH - Two-Part Invention No. 9

HAYDN - Symphony No. 2 ("London")
Allegro spiritoso

BACH - Two-Part Invention No. 6

In Example 2 the interval of inversion in each excerpt is three octaves, one down plus two up in *a*, two down plus one up in *b* and *c*. In actual practice, intervals wider than two octaves are usually spoken of in simpler terms for the sake of convenience, so that the interval of inversion in this case would usually be labeled simply a 15th, or even an octave. In *b* the two outer voices at the start are those concerned in the inversion that follows. Example *c* is continuous; the twin motives are inverted in the second four measures as an answer to the original statement of them in the first four measures.

INVERSION AT INTERVALS OTHER THAN THE OCTAVE

So far we have spoken only about inversion at the octave or multiples of it. Other intervals can sometimes be used successfully, but such arrangements are less likely to be arrived at spontaneously and usually involve a certain amount of testing. Some writers on counterpoint have underlined this distinction by applying the term "natural" to counterpoint invertible at the octave or its multiples and "artificial" to that involving other intervals of inversion.

Among these latter intervals, the 12th and the 10th are the only ones that have been used to any extent by composers, and even the 10th is rare. Other intervals of inversion are of course theoretically possible and may occasionally work out, but their use in music is so infrequent that a discussion of them here seems unwarranted.

In Example 3 the inversion has been effected by transposing the bottom voice up a 5th, and the top voice down an octave. This would of course be referred to as "inversion at the 12th."

EX. 3   BACH - Canonic Variations on "Vom Himmel hoch"

The arrangement in Example 4 is the same, except that the lower of the two inverted voices has been taken up a 12th rather than a 5th and that there is a free third voice at the bottom. Such a voice is sometimes added for purposes of defining the harmonies more clearly, and of improving the contrapuntal effect.

138

EX. 4   BRAHMS - Variations on a Theme by Haydn

Some pairs of voices will invert only at the octave, others at another interval, a few at two different intervals, and a very few at more than two intervals. Example 5 shows a rare instance of a pair of voices that will invert at the octave, the 10th and the 12th. The voices not concerned in the inversion are shown in small notes.

EX. 5   BACH - W. T. C., Vol. II, Fugue 16

Inversion at the 12th

*The original patterns are changed slightly at these points.

Versions *b* and *c* here are not in the same key as *a*, which makes figuring of the interval of inversion more difficult than in preceding examples. In order to have a common key-basis for purposes of comparison, let us transpose the beginning of versions *b* and *c* back to the original key, omitting voices not concerned in the inversion. Example 6 shows this transposition.

EX. 6

It can now be easily seen that in *b* the lower voice has been transposed up a 10th and the upper voice down an octave. There are also certain changes in the inflection of notes because of the use of the major mode in *b*. In *c* the lower voice has been taken up an octave, the upper voice down a 5th. In figuring the interval of inversion we must be careful, in both cases, not to use the changed notes marked with an asterisk.

In Example 7, part *b* is another illustration of inversion at the 10th, Subject II in the tenor of the original version having been transposed that far upward. Version *c* shows a device which amounts to a double inversion; in this case, Subject I, heard as the tenor voice in *b*, appears both a 10th and a 15th higher in *c*. The general principle involved here is that it is usually possible to add a third voice in parallel 3rds or 6ths to either one of the two original voices in counterpoint that is invertible at either the 10th or the 12th.

EX. 7   BACH - The Art of Fugue, No. 10

Original

Inversion
at the 10th

As compared
with (b), in-
version of S. I
at the 15th and
10th; of S. II
at the octave

(S. = Subject)

Notice that in inversion at intervals other than the octave or 15th, the position of whole steps and half steps changes in the inverted melody because the latter begins on a different scale step. Notice, too, that accidentals are frequently introduced in the inverted voice, sometimes to achieve a better melodic line, sometimes to suggest a particular chordal background. Examples 5, 6, and 7 illustrate these points.

GENERAL PRINCIPLES INVOLVED IN WRITING INVERTIBLE COUNTERPOINT

Let us suppose that we are to write a passage invertible at the octave. If we begin as in *a* of Example 8, the attempted inversion, with lower voice transposed up an octave, will turn out as shown in *b*. The voices have not changed places, the higher becoming the lower and *vice versa;* thus no inversion exists.

EX. 8

The same lack of inversion would result if two lines to be inverted at, say, the 10th were more than a 10th apart in their original form. The general principle involved is this: two voices to be inverted must not be separated, in the original version, by more than the interval of the inversion. Consequently, although counterpoint invertible at the octave is also invertible at the 15th, counterpoint written to be invertible at the 15th will not invert at the octave.

The table that follows shows what the various intervals become when inverted at the octave, 10th, and 12th, respectively.

	Inversion at the octave										
Original interval	1	2	3	4	5	6	7	8			
Inverted interval	8	7	6	5	4	3	2	1			

	Inversion at the 10th										
Original interval	1	2	3	4	5	6	7	8	9	10	
Inverted interval	10	9	8	7	6	5	4	3	2	1	

	Inversion at the 12th										
Original interval	1	2	3	4	5	6	7	8	9	10	11	12
Inverted interval	12	11	10	9	8	7	6	5	4	3	2	1

It can be seen from this table why inversion at the 10th is difficult, and consequently rare. The 3rd, 6th, and the 10th, which are the most frequently used intervals, become the octave, the 5th, and the unison, respectively. This tends to give the inverted form a bare, "third-less" sound. Furthermore, parallel 3rds cannot be used in the original version because they become parallel octaves in the inversion (Example 9a); and parallel 6ths are likewise ruled out because they become parallel 5ths (Example 9b).

EX. 9

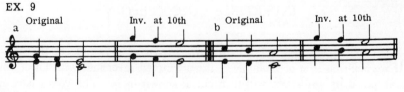

Inversion at the 12th presents no such serious difficulties. The only interval that is likely to cause trouble is the 6th, which becomes a 7th when inverted.

INVERTIBLE COUNTERPOINT INVOLVING THREE OR MORE VOICES

Three-part writing in which the voices are entirely invertible is known as triple counterpoint. It allows for six arrangements of the voices (shown below) although all six are not likely to be used in any one composition. The voices are indicated here by number, 1 standing for the top voice and so on.

$$
\begin{array}{cccccc}
1 & 1 & 2 & 2 & 3 & 3 \\
2 & 3 & 1 & 3 & 1 & 2 \\
3 & 2 & 3 & 1 & 2 & 1
\end{array}
$$

Three arrangements of the voices in a three-voice fugue are shown in the next example. The key is different in each case, and certain small changes are introduced at times, partly to accommodate the tonal entries. Also, voice 1 appears in contrary motion in the bottom version. The voices have been numbered from the top down in *a,* and these numbers are used in the inverted forms to show the various positions of the voices.

EX. 10   BACH - W. T. C., Vol. I, Fugue 21

In quadruple counterpoint the possibilities for different arrangements of the voices are four times as great as in triple counterpoint, a total of twenty-four! Out of this number the composer will of course select only those that happen to work out most naturally.

Completely invertible five-voice writing is extremely rare. However, there is one famous example, certainly one of the most remarkable demonstrations of contrapuntal writing in existence. It occurs in the last movement of Mozart's C major ("Jupiter") Symphony. In the following excerpt, three different arrangements of the voices appear. As before, the voices are numbered so that it will be easy to observe their various positions. Only the string parts are shown in the example, but these include all the essential lines.

EX. 11   MOZART - Symphony No. 41 (K. 551)

SUGGESTED ASSIGNMENTS

1. *Bring in four examples of invertible counterpoint, including at least one in which the inversion is not at the octave or a multiple.*
2. *Write examples of two-voice counterpoint invertible at:*
   a. *the octave (or a multiple)*
   b. *the 10th*
   c. *the 12th*

❧ The Fugue

12

Because fugue offers such rich and varied possibilities for impressive linear writing, it is generally acknowledged to be the apex of contrapuntal technique. If it has sometimes appeared to students to be academic and forbidding, the fault probably lies in the pedantic manner of its presentation. True, fugal procedure is strict and bound by tradition in some respects, yet it is remarkably free in others. And, although there is a tendency to regard the fugue as cold and "abstract," it is capable of conveying a wide variety of moods.

The reader who has covered all the material presented so far in this book will find, as fugue is discussed here, that it involves no principles he has not already encountered, and that it makes frequent use of certain arrangements already familiar, such as invertible counterpoint, stretto, augmentation, diminution and contrary motion.

Before going further, let us consider whether fugue is an actual form, or simply a style or texture. Certainly it was not thought of as a specific form in Bach's day, or even for a full century after his death. But during the late nineteenth century the concept of fugue as a definite three-part form gained acceptance and was furthered by such eminent authorities as Prout and Riemann. Eventually, however, it came to be challenged, disproven, and displaced by the earlier and more valid concept of fugue as a *way* of writing, a particular contrapuntal approach. Consequently, although we sometimes speak of the fugue as "one of the contrapuntal forms," the term "fugue form" is actually meaningless. This is not to say, however, that individual fugues are lacking in a formal plan, nor that the tripartite plan is not frequently encountered. The point is simply that there are various possibilities in fugal architecture, so that it is impossible to single out any one

146

of them as "fugue form." Probably the notion of a set three-part plan for fugues arose because they usually contain:

1) an "exposition," in which the "subject" or main idea is announced in imitative fashion according to a traditional pattern;

2) a freer portion, sometimes called a "development section," which generally avoids the tonic key;

3) some reference to the subject, in the tonic key, near the end. This may be anything from a portion of the subject to a series of complete and emphatic statements, a full-fledged "recapitulation."

The ABA principle is obviously in evidence here in terms of key relationships and, to a greater or lesser degree, in terms of the balancing of the exposition by a similar section near the end. But in determining the "over-all" form of a fugue it is also important to take into account the proportions of the various sections, and their relationship to each other as far as content is concerned. These may clearly indicate a bipartite (or some other non-three-part) design, even though certain suggestions of the ABA feeling may be present. We shall return to the matter of formal analysis later on. In the meantime some of the elements of fugal writing will be considered in detail.

THE SUBJECT

The subject of a fugue differs from an invention motive in that it is likely to be slightly longer and that it is usually announced alone rather than with an accompanying voice as in Bach's three-part inventions. Subjects vary considerably in length, some being as short as one measure, and others as long as eight or more measures. The only principle that applies here is that a subject should be long enough to give the feeling of being an actual line instead of a figure, but not so long that the listener will have difficulty in retaining it. The average length of the subjects in *The Well Tempered Clavier* is probably between two and four measures. The excerpts in Example 1 illustrate a short and a longer subject, respectively.

EX. 1   BACH - W. T. C., Vol. II, Fugue 9

a

BACH - Fugue in G Minor (Organ)

To be interesting as well as readily recognizable when brought back, a subject should have some striking feature, melodic, rhythmic, or both. The subjects shown in Example 2 all possess such features.

EX. 2 · BACH - Fugue in E Minor (Organ)

PURCELL - Sonata No. 7, Canzona

FRESCOBALDI (?) - Fugue

HAYDN - Fifth Mass

BACH - W. T. C., Vol. II, Fugue 6

For instance, in the first of these, the ever-widening interval between the alternating eighth-notes (hence the name "Wedge Fugue") is highly distinctive and makes the subject easily recognizable, even without any unusual rhythmic features to distinguish it. In the beginning of the last subject shown in Example 2, the interest centers in the triplet figure and its opposition to the straight eighth-note rhythm that follows. Melodically, the descending chromatic figure holds our attention. Notice the effective use of sequence in many of these subjects. The corroboration of an element creates a melodic pattern that the ear can grasp, and impresses the material more firmly on the listener's mind.

It need hardly be added that a good subject will have an interesting curve, such as we discussed in Chapter 2. Related to this is the need for a climax point, preferably placed not too near the beginning. As previously mentioned, a sense of climax is not dependent only on pitch, but also on rhythmic factors and harmonic implications. For example, in the following subject the climax point is undoubtedly the A-flat in the second measure, even though it is by no means the highest note.

EX. 3   W. T. C., Vol. I, Fugue 2

(Notice the intentional and effective repetition of a figure here, as well as the "line within a line" formed by the notes that occur at *a, b, c,* and *d.*) On the other hand, the highest note in a melody often *is* the climax point, such as the B on the second beat of the third measure in Example 2*a*.

In this style subjects most often begin on the tonic note, as did all those shown so far. Less frequently they may begin on the fifth or third scale steps, occasionally on the leading-tone if the first note is an anacrusis. In any case, the tonic note must be included near the beginning so that the tonality will be clearly defined. The most successful subjects suggest a solid and interesting harmonic background. A subject may start either on or off the beat, a frequent arrangement being a start after a short rest, as in Examples 3 and 2*b*.

Most fugue subjects do not exceed a range of one octave, and many, especially in four- and five-voice fugues, stay within an even smaller compass.

A subject which can be used in stretto fashion—that is, made to overlap itself at some point—obviously presents more possibilities for interesting development than one that cannot.

THE ANSWER

After the subject has been stated alone, another voice enters and announces it in the dominant. This second announcement is called the "answer." If the fugue has four voices, the fourth announcement will usually be a second answer. Equivalent terms sometimes used instead of statement and answer are *dux* and *comes,* meaning "leader" and "follower" in Latin.

The Fugue

As with the imitation in a three-part invention, the answer in a fugue may be either real or tonal. The principles of real and tonal imitation were discussed in Chapter 8, pages 91–95, and it is assumed that the reader has absorbed that material. A real answer in a fugue is one that imitates the subject exactly, at the perfect 5th. Example 4 illustrates such an answer.

EX. 4   BACH - W.T.C., Vol. I, Fugue 20

In a tonal answer, the dominant note or elements that suggest the dominant harmony are replaced by notes that suggest the original tonic harmony. In other words, those elements are imitated at the 4th instead of at the 5th. Remember that the terms "at the 4th" and "at the 5th" do not always mean literally a 4th above and a 5th above. The notes that would occur at those points may be used in higher or lower octaves instead.

It was pointed out in Chapter 8 that tonal imitation is likely to occur under the following conditions:

1) when the dominant note or the leading tone occurs at or near the beginning of the subject;

2) when the subject modulates to the dominant key.

The first use is illustrated in Example 5. As before, tonal portions are indicated by an X. Example 5c also illustrates the second use.

EX. 5   BACH - W.T.C., Vol. I, Fugue 17

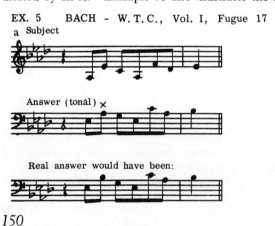

BACH - W.T.C., Vol. II, Fugue 1

b Subject

Answer (tonal)

Real answer would have been: etc.

BACH - W.T.C., Vol. I, Fugue 18

c Subject

Answer (tonal)

Real answer would have been:

In the excerpts shown in Example 6, tonal imitation is involved in the answer because of a modulation to the dominant at the end of the subject. In this style, the dominant key is the only one to which modulations within subjects are made.

EX. 6   BACH - C Major Fugue (Organ)

a Subject

Answer (tonal)

Real answer would have been:

BACH - W. T. C., Vol. I, Fugue 7

Curiously enough, this use of tonal imitation applies even when a modulation to the dominant at the end of the subject proper is followed by a return to the tonic key within a group of link tones, as in Example 6*b*. Notice that the answer to a modulating subject normally begins in the new key but must end in the old key (the original tonic). This is of course just the reverse of what happens in the subject itself.

Occasionally the dominant element recurs so constantly throughout a subject that tonal imitation of the entire subject becomes necessary. This can be seen in Example 7.

EX. 7   BACH - Fugue in D Minor (Organ)

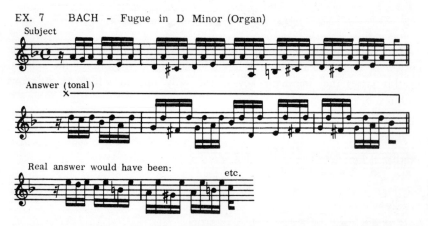

It may do no harm to reiterate a point made earlier. Tonal imitation is generally avoided when it would destroy some characteristic or distinctive melodic pattern in the subject. For instance, the subject of the "Little" G minor Fugue of Bach opens with an outline of the tonic triad. This pattern is preserved in the answer, so that it is a real one despite the strong dominant note on the second beat.

EX. 8   BACH - Fugue in G Minor (Organ)

Even in such cases, however, it is not always possible to predict whether a real or a tonal answer will be used. The musical situation in Example 9 seems to be very similar to that in Example 8, yet Bach employs a tonal answer.

EX. 9   BACH - Musical Offering

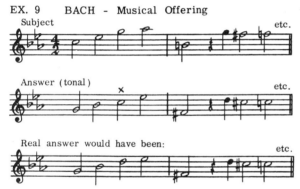

Much has been written about tonal imitation, its varied use by composers of different periods, and the reasons that first brought it into being. The most important reason seems to have been a desire to extend the feeling of the tonic key into the answer. In fact, the tonic feeling may sometimes persist through much of the answer. Such an arrangement is likely to suggest itself if the subject is short, for in such cases a departure into the dominant key soon after the beginning might seem too sudden, thereby breaking up the musical pattern into undesirably short segments.

A point made by most writers on fugue has been neatly expressed by Tovey: "The question arises whether the alternation between subject and answer is an alternation between *two keys* or an alternation between *two positions of the same scale.*" * The latter effect is often closer to what we

* Tovey, Sir Donald, *Musical Textures*.   London: Oxford University Press, p. 65.

hear when tonal imitation is used.

It has also been suggested that this concept of two different positions of the same scale harks back to the system of modes, in which each mode had its hypo-mode, the difference between mode and hypo-mode being essentially one of range.

THE THREE-VOICE FUGUE EXPOSITION

The initial statement of the subject and answer in all voices in turn is called the exposition.* Usually there are as many announcements in the exposition as there are voices in the fugue, although an extra announcement is sometimes added.

In order to work with actual music rather than in the abstract, let us examine, in Example 10, the exposition of a three-voice fugue from *The Well Tempered Clavier.*

EX. 10   BACH - W. T. C.,   Vol. I,   Fugue 2

---

* The word "exposition" has been used by some writers on fugue to mean any announcement of the subject, at the beginning or later. But the more restricted meaning given above is the one generally understood today, and it has therefore been adopted here.

154

Link passage based on begin. of S. and on C. S. I in contrary motion

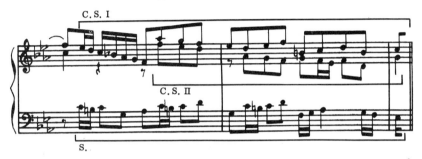

C. S. I

C. S. II

S.

The subject, in C minor, starts on the tonic note in the middle voice after an eighth rest, and extends through the first sixteenth note in the third measure. Certain points concerning the construction of the subject were mentioned earlier on page 149. The answer in the top voice, beginning on the second eighth note of the third measure, is tonal as might be expected, in view of the dominant note, G, near the start of the subject. C is substituted for D, that note being the only one changed in the tonal answer. When the dominant note occurs *later* in the subject it receives a real answer. Notice that the key of the answer is G minor, not G major. Although the dominant chord in a minor key is usually major, the dominant *key* of a minor key is minor.

The middle voice continues against the answer with a new melodic line called, in this case, a "counter-subject." A counter-subject is a melodic idea that appears consistently along with the subject in the exposition—from the second announcement on, of course, since the first is unaccompanied—and later in the fugue as well. A counter-subject must also have melodic interest, individuality, and enough rhythmic contrast to make it a good foil for the subject, yet the two must make a natural and satisfying combination. As Oldroyd somewhat romantically puts it, "The two must *belong to each other.*" * A counter-subject and its subject must also be invertible; that is, each must work well as upper or lower voice.

* Oldroyd, George, *The Technique and Spirit of Fugue.* London: Oxford University Press, 1948, p. 38.

Some fugues do not make use of a counter-subject. In such cases the voice that accompanies the subject is referred to simply as "free voice" or "accompanying voice." This arrangement is seen more often in four-voice fugues and will be illustrated in connection with them.

At the beginning of the fifth measure the key is still the dominant, and an announcement in the tonic key at that point without preparation would obviously be crude and unmusical. Consequently, Bach uses the next two measures for a return to C minor, effected by means of sequential extension of the head of the subject. Link passages of this sort, discussed earlier in connection with inventions, occur even more frequently in fugues. Most of them involve extension of material just heard, as is the case here.

In the seventh measure the bottom voice takes the subject, the top voice takes the first counter-subject, and the middle voice has another melodic idea. The middle voice begins later than the other two and is not highly independent, starting as it does in parallel 3rds with the first counter-subject. It is nevertheless a clearly defined melodic element that returns several times in the course of the fugue; consequently it should undoubtedly be called a second counter-subject rather than simply "free voice." A regularly recurring second counter-subject can also be seen in Example 10, in Chapter 11, page 143, the line labeled "2."

This much of the fugue (measures 1–9) constitutes the exposition. As previously mentioned, some three-voice fugue expositions include a fourth announcement of the subject in the dominant, so that the aural effect is that of a four-voice fugue exposition with one voice dropping out in the fourth announcement (e.g., *The Well Tempered Clavier*, Volume I, Fugues 8, 19, 21). The inclusion of an extra fifth announcement in four-voice fugues is much more rarely encountered.

In three-voice fugues the order of keys in the exposition is always tonic, dominant, tonic. The voices may enter (taking the subject) in various orders. If we employ our usual system of numbering the voices from top to bottom, the regular orders of entry may be expressed as follows:

123   213   231   321

(In Example 10 the order was 213.) The term "regular" is applied to those orders in which the statement in an even-numbered voice is followed by the answer in an odd-numbered voice or *vice versa*. Of the many three-voice fugues in *The Well Tempered Clavier*, only Numbers 3 and 4 in Volume II use an irregular order, 312. The orders 321 and 231, while regular, are rare.

The plan of the three-voice fugue exposition is as follows, the order 123 having been arbitrarily chosen.

EX. 11

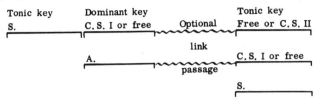

It should perhaps be mentioned that when an exposition is extended beyond the normal proportions shown here, either by the addition of an announcement or by sequential extension, the cadence at the end of it usually occurs in a key other than the tonic. Fugues 6 and 8 in the first volume of *The Well Tempered Clavier* are among those that demonstrate this possibility.

THE FOUR-VOICE FUGUE EXPOSITION

As might be expected, the exposition in a four-voice fugue simply carries one step further the pattern we observed in three-voice fugues. The excerpt shown here is a fairly typical example.

EX. 12   BACH - W. T. C., Vol. I, Fugue 23

Although no "link passage" is present here between the second and third announcements of the subject, such passages are frequent in four-voice fugues, as they are in the three-voice variety (see Example 10, Chapter 13, page 176).

Once again we can observe the use of tonal imitation in the third and seventh measures, caused in this case by the presence of the leading tone (A-sharp) near the beginning of the subject, and the notes C-sharp and F-sharp shortly after that.

The order of entry here happens to be tenor, alto, soprano, bass, or in terms of numbers, 3214. The regular orders of entry in four-voice fugues are the following:

1234	2143	3214
4321	2341	3412

As in three-voice fugues, an order is considered regular if an odd-numbered voice is answered by an even-numbered voice or *vice versa*, and if the first two announcements are in adjacent voices. Other orders which are possible but irregular are:

2134	3241

It can be seen that in a regular order and in the usual arrangement of alternating tonic and dominant keys, the announcement of the subject in the soprano is an octave above that in the tenor, while the same relationship exists between the alto and the bass announcements.

158

In Example 12, as in most four-voice fugue expositions, the pattern of key relationships is tonic, dominant, tonic, dominant. Another pattern is possible and is seen occasionally: tonic, dominant, dominant, tonic. Example 13 illustrates this arrangement as well as the irregular order 2134 mentioned earlier.

EX. 13   BACH - W.T.C., Vol. I, Fugue 1

The majority of four-voice fugues make use of one or more counter-subjects. The fugue in Example 12, for instance, has a counter-subject, starting with descending sixteenth notes, that first appears in the tenor line in the third measure, and is taken by the alto against the third announcement of the subject, and by the soprano against the fourth announcement. Although the whole of this melodic line does not recur frequently in the course of the fugue, the beginning of it does, and this fact plus the repeated use of the line intact in the exposition and its reappearance at the end, seem sufficient justification for calling it a counter-subject.

Second counter-subjects are infrequent, and the use of a third counter-subject in a four-voice fugue is extremely rare. In the first place, that voice is usually present, in the exposition, during only one announcement of the subject. Consequently, one of the criteria for determining whether it *is* a counter-subject, namely its reappearance with the subject, is missing. The term "third counter-subject" is probably appropriate only in rare cases where the material returns frequently in later portions of the fugue.

Not all fugues make use of a counter-subject. The beginning of one that does not is shown in Example 14.

EX. 14   BACH - W. T. C., Vol. I, Fugue 5

a4.

The absence of a counter-subject here is offset by the distinctive and arresting character of the subject itself, as well as by its shortness.

Other fugues in the first volume of *The Well Tempered Clavier* that do not use a counter-subject are numbers 1, 8, 17, and 22. A further illustration from the twelfth fugue in the second volume can be seen in Example 17.

Example 15 shows the general plan of the exposition in a four-voice fugue. Where a first counter-subject or free material could be used, "C.S. I" is listed first, inasmuch as a counter-subject is encountered more often than free material at that point. On the other hand, second and third counter-subjects are *less* usual than free material. "Free" is therefore listed first when one or the other could be involved.

EX. 15

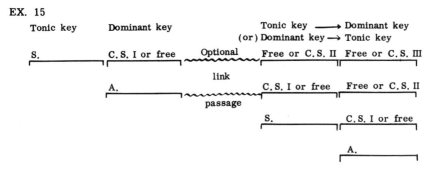

THE SUBJECT AS RELATED TO THE MATERIAL THAT FOLLOWS IT

In most fugues the point at which the subject ends and the counter-subject or free material begins is quite clear. It may be marked by at least a mild cadential feeling, though there is generally no pause in the rhythmic motion, or by some new melodic or rhythmic element. Example 12 illustrates both these features. However, in cases where neither of these guideposts is present, the beginning of the counter-subject may be difficult if not impossible to fix exactly. Consider this fugue, for example:

EX. 16   BACH - W. T. C., Vol. I,   Fugue 9

Here the first statement of the subject could be heard as extending through the G-sharp on the second beat of the second measure, or through the B which is also the first note of the answer. Or, if one hears it as extending

161

well beyond the middle of the second measure, this is then an example of the "stretto fugue." This type of fugue will be dealt with shortly.

The fact that this and certain other points in connection with fugue cannot always be pinned down with a hard-and-fast analysis should not be a matter of concern to us. A great deal of time can be wasted in debating what Tovey has called "vexatious minutiae." The important thing, rather, is to glean from a study of fugue the broad underlying principles of the musical structure. In the particular case at hand, the very fact that we sometimes have difficulty determining exactly where the subject ends should tell us that in good fugue writing the subject generally flows smoothly into the counter-subject, the two often forming a continuous line.

As in three-part inventions, the end of the subject proper is sometimes followed by a melodic link consisting of one or more notes that generally move scalewise, and perform the functions of keeping the rhythm going and of leading smoothly to the first note of the counter-subject or free material. The fugue which follows contains a good example.

EX. 17   BACH - W. T. C., Vol. II, Fugue 12

Mel. link

Here the subject proper seems to end with the A-flat at the beginning of the fourth full measure, the rest of the notes in that measure being link-tones of lesser importance.

As mentioned earlier, there is no counter-subject in this fugue.

This example provides a further illustration of a link passage (measures 9–11) between the second and third announcements of the subject.

THE SUBJECT AS RELATED TO THE ANSWER; THE STRETTO FUGUE

From the examples given so far it can be seen that in the two most usual arrangements the answer begins either immediately following the last note of the subject or along with that note. Only rarely is it appropriate to analyze the answer as overlapping the subject by more than one or two notes. Yet that analysis seems necessary in fugues such as the one quoted in Example 18, where the ear receives a definite impression that the answer has begun before the subject has been completed.

EX. 18   BACH - W. T. C., Vol. II, Fugue 3

con. mot.

con. mot.

163

Fugues that begin in this fashion are sometimes referred to as "stretto fugues."

SPECIAL DEVICES AS USED IN THE EXPOSITION

Augmentation, diminution and contrary motion, like stretto, appear only rarely in the exposition of fugues. In Example 18 the third announcement of the subject is in contrary motion. The same principle is carried even further in Example 19, where all the announcements after the initial one are in contrary motion. Such a fugue is known as a "counter-fugue" (*Gegenfuge* in German). Example 19 also illustrates the use of other devices in an exposition. The first statement of the subject is in diminution, as compared with the original form used earlier in *The Art of Fugue*, and the same is true of the announcement beginning in measure 3. The last announcement, measure 5 in the bottom voice, uses augmentation; there is even a hint of double diminution in the last measure; and stretto is present throughout.

EX. 19   BACH - The Art of Fugue, No. 7

Aug., con. mot.

(Double dim.)

Of course such a concentration of devices is highly unusual. It occurs in this case as part of Bach's virtuoso demonstration of the possibilities in fugue writing.

THE COUNTER-EXPOSITION

In some fugues the regular exposition is followed, often after a short episodic passage, by a second exposition, called a "counter-exposition." Although the plan of keys in this section is sometimes the same as in the main exposition, the order of entry of the voices is usually different. Among the fugues in *The Well Tempered Clavier*, the following contain counter-expositions:

Volume I, Fugues 1 and 11

Volume II, Fugues 9, 17 and 23 (the last with partial counter-exposition)

Occasionally the subject is announced in the tonic key in the middle portion of a fugue, and in some treatises on counterpoint this is also called a counter-exposition. The author feels that the term is better reserved for a series of statements involving the tonic and dominant as at the beginning. Obviously the question here is merely one of semantics.

The Fugue

SUGGESTED ASSIGNMENTS

Page in
Workbook

1. *Analyze fugue expositions as specified by the instructor. This will of course include a detailed examination of the subject, and of the counter-subject if one is present, singly and in combination.*

2. *Write answers to the fugue subjects given in the Workbook.*　　57

3. *Using one of the subjects given in the Workbook, write the exposition of a three-voice fugue.*　　57

4. *Using one of the subjects given in the Workbook, write the exposition of a four-voice fugue.*　　57

5. *Write six fugue subjects. Make them as varied as possible.*

6. *Using one of these original subjects, write the exposition of a three-voice fugue.*

7. *Using one of these original subjects, write the exposition of a four-voice fugue.*

The Fugue (Continued)

13

Only the exposition of a fugue proceeds according to a set formal plan; what happens after that is dictated by the nature of the musical material, and by the taste and imagination of the composer. The general procedure is to bring the subject back in various keys and in various voices, usually with episodes between these announcements. The subject in its complete form is seldom announced twice in succession in the same voice. Contrapuntal devices and interchange of the voices are often used to create interest and variety. At or near the end of the fugue there is usually at least one announcement of the subject in the tonic key, often more. Sometimes a short coda is added. The structure of the whole is generally sectional, with cadences marking the ends of sections. It must be stressed, however, that at such cadence points there is no pronounced halt in the rhythmic motion as there often is in the homophonic forms. Sometimes a suspension or passing tone in one voice carries on the rhythmic flow, or a musical idea in one of the lines may extend through and beyond the cadence point. Such devices tend to soften the dividing action of the cadence, and provide the sense of continuity that is so important in fugal writing.

Let us now examine some of these features.

EPISODES

In a fugue, an episode is a passage in which the subject does not appear intact, though fragments of it are often involved. Episodes may also be derived from a counter-subject, occasionally from other material. They may even introduce new material, provided it is in keeping with the character of the fugue and is corroborated at other points. Their main functions are to effect a smooth transition between one key and the next, and to provide variety, as well as relief from constant emphasis on the subject as a whole. Almost invariably, episodes are accorded sequential treatment. In fact, the importance of the sequence in fugue cannot be over-stressed. Another device often used is the interchange of voices, either within a single episode or between one episode and another.

Let us see, now, how these points apply in some characteristic episodes from a Bach fugue. Example 10 in Chapter 12, page 154, showed the exposition of the well-known C minor fugue from the first volume of *The Well Tempered Clavier*. In Example 1 that follows, the first episode shown begins at the point where the example on page 155 ended.

EX. 1   BACH - W. T. C., Vol. I, Fugue 2

In the first of these episodes a fragment from the beginning of the subject is tossed back and forth between the upper two voices, while the lower voice elaborates on the first counter-subject. Sequential treatment is very much in evidence. In the course of the two measures a modulation from the tonic key, C minor, to the relative major, E-flat, is effected via the circle of 5ths.

In *b* the top voice derives from the first counter-subject in contrary motion, the bottom voices from a portion of the first counter-subject—or from a similar group of notes at the beginning of the second counter-subject. Key-wise, we progress again around the circle of 5ths from E-flat major to C minor, but this time in the opposite direction. Once more, sequence is important.

In *c,* fragments of the subject appear in the outer voices against a portion of the counter-subject in contrary motion in the inner voice. As before, the treatment is sequential. The two bottom voices here have an inverted version of the link passage between measures 5 and 6. This excerpt provides an excellent illustration of the interchange of voices within an episode, the interchange taking place just after the middle of the second measure. A shift in key is also involved in this case. The bottom voice is shifted up a 4th to become the middle voice, while the original middle voice appears a 12th lower as the bottom voice. The original top voice remains the top voice but is shifted down a 5th to fit the new key. Although we seem to be modulating during each of these measure-and-half segments, in each case the chromatic progression brings us back to the same key we left. The real modulation occurs suddenly at the point where the voices interchange.

As a rule, the texture in episodes is thinned out as compared with the preceding and following parts. In four and five-voice fugues it is highly unusual for all the voices to continue during an episode, and often all but two are allowed to drop out temporarily. The same is true even in three-voice fugues. This is still another way in which episodes can provide welcome variety—that is, through lightening of the texture.

It is somewhat surprising to find that the very first fugue of *The Well Tempered Clavier* contains no episodes, since that situation is highly unusual.

The Fugue (Continued)

In such cases, other devices must take the place of episodes in providing new interest and relief from too many consecutive statements of the subject in its original form.

MIDDLE ENTRIES

The term "middle entries," though more literally accurate in fugues of three-part design, seems to be a convenient one for describing those announcements of the subject that occur after the exposition, but before the final return to the tonic key. In the C minor fugue quoted earlier in the chapter, there are two such middle entries, one between episodes *a* and *b* of Example 1, the other between episodes *b* and *c*.

EX. 2   BACH - W. T. C., Vol. I, Fugue 2

The first of these entries is in E-flat, the relative major key, in the top voice. The second is in G minor, the dominant key, in the middle voice, and is tonal (C instead of D for the fourth note). In the middle entries Bach generally confines himself to the five closely related keys listed in Chapter 6, page 62.

Notice the economy of means shown by Bach here in Example 2. The

170

two counter-subjects are used against the subject each time, but their position as different voices keeps them fresh and interesting. This is an impressive illustration of the usefulness and effectiveness of invertible counterpoint.

In fugues that do not have as extensive a final portion as this one, there are likely to be more middle entries, though their number is also influenced by such considerations as the number and length of the episodes, and the length of the subject.

SPECIAL DEVICES AS APPLIED TO THE MIDDLE ENTRIES

Stretto, augmentation, diminution and contrary motion appear very frequently in fugal writing, stretto being especially common. Retrograde motion, however, is rarely encountered. Although these devices may occur anywhere in the fugue, even in the exposition, they are particularly characteristic of the middle entries, and it is this use with which we are concerned at the moment. Example 3 shows:

1) in *a*, the subject of a fugue;

2) in *b*, stretto involving the upper two voices;

3) in *c*, the subject stated in contrary motion in the middle voice;

4) in *d*, contrary motion in the two upper voices plus augmentation (with some changes in the relative rhythmic values) in the top voice; also stretto at the 5th between these voices;

5) in *e*, stretto involving all three voices, with the subject first in its normal form, then in contrary motion.

EX. 3   BACH - W. T. C., Vol. I, Fugue 8

a Subject

b measures 19-22

c measures 36-38

d measures 47-49

e measures 52-55

The excerpt that follows is a further example of Bach's amazing contrapuntal dexterity.

EX. 4   BACH - W.T.C., Vol. II, Fugue 2

Here three different forms of the subject appear, the normal form in the top voice, an augmented version in the middle voice, and one using contrary motion in the bottom voice.

Another useful and fairly frequent device in fugal composition is the pedal point. In general, pedal points occur more often near the ends of fugues than earlier, but those that do appear in the middle portions are almost invariably of the dominant variety. This is the case in Example 5, the key at that point being D minor.

EX. 5   BACH - W. T. C., Vol. I, Fugue 11

THE FINAL PORTION

Because fugues are constructed in different ways, it is no more possible to lay down a set plan for the final portion than it was for the middle portion. Even the use of the terms "middle portion" and "final portion" could be criticized as implying a distinct three-part division which, as pointed out earlier, is by no means always present in terms of total form. There are, however, certain specific devices that should be mentioned in connection with the closing portions of fugues.

First of all, in this style there will invariably be a return to the tonic key somewhere before the end. If the fugue has a full recapitulation, the point of return is likely to be about two-thirds of the way through. Otherwise it may not be reached until much nearer the end. When we speak of a recapitulation, we do not mean a literal repetition of the exposition, but rather a similar section in which the subject and counter-subject, if any, appear—but generally with voices interchanged or with some other difference. The last announcement of the subject, either at the very end or just before the coda, is usually given to an outer voice, either top or bottom, so that it will be heard prominently. In Example 6, again from the C minor fugue in Volume I, *a* is the first announcement of the subject in the recapitulation and *b* is another statement before a brief coda (shown in Example 9), which presents a final, harmonized version of the subject over a pedal point.

EX. 6   BACH - W. T. C., Vol. I, Fugue 2

Once again we cannot help being impressed by the number of interesting rearrangements of material achieved by Bach through the skillful interchanging of parts.   It need hardly be added that such an approach will be successful only if the original material is strong, and if it lends itself to treatment as invertible counterpoint.

Some fugues have only a short recapitulation, possibly no more than a single statement of the subject.   In rare cases only a portion of the subject is brought back.

Strettos in the closing portions of fugues can be extremely effective.   A good example is the one beginning in measure 28 of Example 10, and another was shown in Example 14 in Chapter 9, page 107.   That excerpt also illustrates another possibility, the use of augmentation during the final announcements of the subject.   Possibly the most impressive final stretto in *The Well Tempered Clavier* is the one from the Fugue in B-flat minor in the first volume, part of which was shown in Example 9, Chapter 9, page 104.

As already mentioned, pedal points most often appear in the latter portions of fugues.   If they occur before the coda, they are nearly always on the dominant. In the example that follows, the dominant pedal point is decorated.

EX. 7   BACH - W. T. C., Vol. II, Fugue 10

Another device that Bach is fond of bringing in near the end of a fugue is that of "added 3rds," which is illustrated in the next example. A contrapuntal *tour de force*, this passage involves the subject, with added 3rds, in stretto with the subject in contrary motion, also with added 3rds!

EX. 8   BACH - W. T. C., Vol. II, Fugue 22

When a coda is included at the end of a fugue, it may be anything from a few beats to several measures long, seldom more than four measures. It may either use material heard previously or introduce new material, or both. The codas of many Bach fugues show a tendency toward a freer, more rhapsodical treatment, in some cases even toward a dramatic *recitative* style.

175

The Fugue (Continued)

Extra voices are often added at this point for the sake of increased sonority; and a full chord at the end is usual. Codas frequently make use of tonic pedal points. That is the case in Example 9, once more from the C minor fugue previously quoted.

EX. 9   BACH - W. T. C., Vol. I, Fugue 2

THE FUGUE AS A WHOLE

So far we have approached fugue in a rather piece-meal fashion. The reader should make it a particular point to study the C minor fugue from Volume I that has been quoted so often in this chapter. He will then see how the various elements we have discussed relate to each other, and to the total plan.

It may be helpful now to consider one fugue as a whole. With that in mind, the G minor fugue from the first volume of *The Well Tempered Clavier* is given next. Analytical markings have been added in the music, and other comments follow.

EX. 10   BACH - W. T. C., Vol. I, Fugue 16

The Fugue (Continued)

Episode using end of S., C.S.

The Fugue (Continued)

The subject of this fugue is a good example of what some writers have called the "head-and-tail" type—that is, a subject that has two distinct and somewhat contrasting parts. It is first stated in the alto and is a measure and a half long. Since it begins on the fifth scale step we would expect a tonal answer to be used, and that proves to be the case when the soprano enters in the second measure. Only the first note, G, has been changed as compared with a real answer, which would have called for an A at that point. Against this answer the first voice has a counter-subject which begins with material from the end of the subject in contrary motion. In the fourth measure the answer is extended sequentially to form a link passage that leads back to G minor. The bass then announces the subject an octave lower than the first statement in the alto, while the other voices continue. Finally, the tenor enters with a tonal answer, the notes being an octave lower than those in the soprano answer. Technically, this is the end of the exposition. However, the four-measure episode that follows could be heard as an addition to the exposition, especially since it leads back to G minor on the way, and involves a clear-cut cadence in that key before proceeding to the relative key, B-flat major.

The construction of the rest of the fugue can be seen from the analytical notes that have been added. Consequently, it seems unnecessary to comment measure-by-measure, although there are some features that merit special notice. These are as follows:

1) Rests are present from time to time in each voice. These give a sense of "breathing" and a clear-cut delineation of the separate segments of the music. Furthermore, a constant use of four-voice texture would become monotonous; thus the dropping out of a voice for at least a measure or two now and then provides relief, and also makes the voice doubly effective when it re-enters. Important statements of the subject are therefore often preceded by a rest in the voice involved. Actually, a good portion of this fugue, and of many four-voice fugues, makes use of only three voices rather than four. This is an important point to remember, since students often make the mistake of attempting to keep all four voices going throughout a fugue, thereby making their task unnecessarily difficult and the result less effective than it might have been. On the other hand, the dropping out of a voice before the end of the exposition, which occurs in this fugue, is somewhat unusual. Students should follow the normal plan of having all the voices

continue at least through the exposition.

2) The keys used for the middle entries in measures 12 and 24 are:

B-flat major (relative major): measure 12 to the middle of measure 13.

F major (dominant of the relative major): two announcements, the first tonal; the middle of measure 13 to the middle of measure 16. These have the character of answers in relation to the preceding B-flat major announcements.

B-flat major (relative major); measure 17 to the middle of measure 18; in stretto with the next announcement.

F major (dominant of the relative major); slightly altered; the middle of measure 17 to the beginning of measure 19.

C minor (subdominant); two announcements, measure 20 to the beginning of measure 23.

G minor (tonic, or, as first heard here, the dominant of the subdominant key); measure 23 to the middle of measure 24. The effect here is that of a tonal answer in relation to the C minor statements heard just previously. Although in most cases the return to the tonic key signals the final section or recapitulation of a fugue, this G minor announcement has more the character of another middle entry. The actual recapitulation, then, does not begin until measure 28.

3) Notes may be added to the subject or counter-subject, as in measure 23, where a passing-note D is added between C and E-flat in the middle voice, and in measure 24, where D and B-flat are added between the E-flat, C and A of the counter-subject.

4) In measures 7 and 11 there are "false entries," passages that suggest the subject at first, but then depart from it.

5) When false entries are involved in a stretto, it is called a "mock stretto." An example occurs here in measure 7.

6) Notice the dramatic and forceful quality of the stretto that begins seven measures from the end. Bach has carefully avoided the head of the subject for several measures before that, so that it will be fresh and arresting when it enters again.

7) Voices have been added during the closing measures. The treatment becomes more straightforwardly harmonic at that point.

8) If we divide this fugue (Example 10) into its component sections, we arrive at the following:

The Fugue (Continued)

Measure numbers		Number of measures
1–7	Four announcements of the subject	7
8–11	Episode	4
12–16	Three announcements of the subject	5
mid. 16–end 16	Episode (extension)	½
17–18	The subject in stretto *	2
19	Episode *	1
20–mid. 24	Three announcements of the subject	4½
mid. 24–27	Episode	3½
28–29	Three announcements of the subject in stretto, the last incomplete (tonic)	2
30–mid. 31	Episode	1½
mid. 31–end	Two announcements of the subject (tonic)	3½

* These two portions overlap each other by half a measure; that is, the episode actually begins a half measure earlier than shown, against the close of the stretto portion.

If the measures from the final stretto to the end of the fugue are grouped as one unit balancing the exposition, we shall find a surprisingly symmetrical arrangement in this fugue. The mid-point is, of course, the brief stretto beginning in measure 17, and it is appropriate that the climax of the fugue in terms of pitch should be reached during that passage. The terms "arch form" and "bow form," which are often applied to fugues in ABA design, seem especially fitting here.

THE SCHOLASTIC FUGUE

The fugue shown in Example 10 comes closer than most of those in *The Well Tempered Clavier* to resembling the "scholastic" ("textbook" or "student") fugue in plan. Nevertheless, the symmetry of design in this fugue and the fact that the voices do not continue through the exposition, are exceptional.

The scholastic fugue is a synthetic model developed long ago by pedagogues for their students to emulate. The following table of suggested contents, keys and proportions is given by Gedalge in his massive *Traité de la Fugue*. It is intended to apply to a four-voice fugue with a subject four to six measures in length.

182

Designation of the parts of the fugue	Number of measures varying approximately	
	from	*to*
Exposition	16	24
First episode	8	12
Subject in the submediant	4	6
Answer (mediant)	4	6
Second episode	10	16
Subject in the subdominant	4	6
Transition	2	4
Subject or answer in the supertonic	4	6
Third episode	14	20
From the beginning of the fugue to the stretto	66	100

This plan takes the fugue only up to the final stretto, for which Gedalge suggests another 44 to 50 measures. He explains that there is nothing arbitrary about the numbers of measures given here, that they are to be regarded merely as estimated extremes for a student fugue. It might be pointed out that even the minimum proportions suggested for the fugue as a whole are large as compared with those of most fugues in *The Well Tempered Clavier*. Also, within the fugue, the final stretto recommended seems abnormally long. The reason for this is presumably that the student is expected to demonstrate several different types of stretto. Gedalge lists three of these:

1) the usual type in which canonic entrances of the subject succeed each other without interruption;

2) that in which the stretto announcements of the subject and answer are separated by stretto announcements of the counter-subject;

3) that in which episodes separate the stretto announcements of the subject and answer.

The keys specified in the table above apply only when the subject is in major, a different succession being recommended when the subject is in minor.

Obviously, the plan of the scholastic fugue is a highly artificial one. Few if any fugues in musical literature correspond with it. Furthermore, there exists a certain danger in using it,—namely that students will begin to think of it as a kind of standard plan, whereas an examination of fugal literature will show that there is no "standard plan." Yet it may have some value in the beginning stages of fugal writing, when students sometimes find themselves at a loss as to procedure unless they have some sort of blue-print to guide them. If it *is* used, the author recommends that the over-all proportions suggested by Gedalge be drastically reduced.

The Fugue (Continued)

OTHER TYPES OF FUGAL DESIGN

It has been pointed out that by no means all fugues are built according to a three-part plan. Space does not permit the illustration of other types of design, but examples from *The Well Tempered Clavier* will be mentioned, and the student should inspect them. Fugues involving more than one subject, and those with more than four voices or fewer than three voices, will be discussed in the next chapter.

Most fugues that fall into two portions are separated near the middle by a decided cadence. The opening of the second portion is often marked by some new treatment, such as contrary motion, or the introduction of a new counterpoint. Those features can be seen in the following examples of bipartite design, all from *The Well Tempered Clavier*:

Volume I, Fugue 14 (Part I to measure 20; Part II begins with the subject in contrary motion in the alto).

Volume II, Fugue 2 (Part I to measure 14; Part II includes augmentation and the addition of a fourth voice).

Volume II, Fugue 7 (Part I to measure 30).

A special case is the two-voice fugue in E minor, Number 10 in the first volume. Although it contains no actual cadence at the mid-point and no startling change in treatment at the beginning of the second half, it is perhaps the most plainly bipartite of all the fugues in *The Well Tempered Clavier*. With the exception of four bars of coda, the whole second half, starting in measure 20, is simply a transposition of the first half, with the voices interchanged. The coda consists mainly of two partial statements of the subject in the tonic key.

Siegmund Levarie analyzes thirteen of the fugues in the first volume of *The Well Tempered Clavier* as being essentially bipartite.* However, he points out that six of these contain short recapitulations, and this comment brings us to a question that inevitably arises in the analysis of fugues: how much of a recapitulation may be present without giving the form a preponderantly three-part (ABA) feeling rather than a bipartite feeling? Since there seems to be no way of providing a hard and fast answer to this question,

---

* Levarie, Siegmund, *Fugue and Form*. Copyright by Siegmund Levarie, 1941. Levarie makes extensive use of the concept of "bar form," the plan of which is normally *a a | b*, the *b* part being about as long as the two *a*'s together. The two *a*'s are not necessarily alike, but need be only broadly similar. As this concept, involving German terms for the sections, is unfamiliar to most American students, it has not been employed here, although Dr. Levarie makes a good case for its use in fugal analysis.

184

and since the answer may vary from person to person, there is obviously some leeway in classifying fugues as two-part or three-part. For example, we find Goetschius classifying Fugue 17 in Volume I as two-part, while Levarie considers it to be three-part. Levarie also cites Fugue 8 in Volume I as an example of a doubtful case which could be classified either way.

Certain fugues, such as Number 12 in Volume I, seem to fit into neither the two-part nor the three-part categories, and can only be described as "sectional."

One particular type of fugal design, seen in Fugue 19 of Volume I, needs separate mention, not only because it represents a special case, but because it gives some interesting insight into fugal technique of an earlier period. Levarie calls it "strophic form" and has this to say about it:

> The form of this fugue, rare in Bach, reminds us of the older technique of Sweelinck. A century before Bach, on the path leading from the early ricercar to the maturer fugue, Sweelinck had tied together the various sections of the ricercar by retaining one main subject throughout the composition. The counterpoints to that subject changed with every new section, and made them sound like separate fugues upon the same subject.*

A further example of this same general technique can be seen in Fugue 4 of Volume I. This fugue is sometimes even listed as a ricercar (or ricercare). The same is true of the famous "St. Anne" Fugue.

This approach may involve any number of sections. In the case of Fugues 4 and 19 cited above, there are three. In Number 19, a characteristic rhythm in each section makes the ternary form especially clear.

SUGGESTED ASSIGNMENTS

Page in
Workbook

1. Analyze fugues as specified by the instructor.

2. Write short stretto passages based on the subjects in the Workbook (bottom of the page).   57

3. Complete the three-voice fugue on a given subject, begun earlier as an assignment in connection with Chapter 12.

4. Complete the three-voice fugue on an original subject begun earlier.

5. Complete the four-voice fugue on a given subject, begun earlier.

6. Complete the four-voice fugue on an original subject, begun earlier.

* *Ibid.*, p. 28.

❧ *The Fugue (Concluded)*

14

THE FIVE-VOICE FUGUE

The subject of a five-voice fugue is likely to be slow-moving and dignified in character, for the obvious reason that a faster subject might present too much of a technical problem, at least on keyboard instruments, when so many voices are involved. There are only two five-voice fugues in *The Well Tempered Clavier*. In one, Number 4 of Volume I, the bottom voice enters first with the subject, then the next lowest voice enters, and so on, the order being 54321 in terms of the numbering system we have used before. In the other, Number 22 of Volume I, the order of entry is the reverse, or 12345.

Whatever the order of entry, the sequence of announcements in a five-voice fugue should be: subject, answer, subject, answer, subject, or I V I V I in terms of keys. Each "subject" will be an octave higher or lower than the preceding "subject," and the same is true of the "answers."

Here is the beginning of the first five-voice fugue mentioned above, a triple fugue, incidentally, which is referred to again on page 193:

EX. 1   BACH - W. T. C., Vol. I, Fugue 4

The fourth entry here, starting in measure 12, is irregular. It is actually in the subdominant, the G-sharp at the beginning being a substitute for F-sharp.

FUGUES OF SIX OR MORE VOICES

As might be expected, fugues involving six or more voices are extremely uncommon. Not only is it difficult to handle that many parts, both in composition and in performance, but clarity of individual line becomes harder to maintain as the number of voices increases. The danger, therefore, is that the effect may prove more harmonic than contrapuntal. Of course in works that do use this many voices, rests of considerable length are frequent, so that the texture is kept from being too consistently thick.

Examples of six-voice fugues
Bach, Organ Compositions, Vol. VI,* No. 13.
Bach, Musical Offering, No. 5, Ricercare a 6.
Bach, B-minor Mass, No. 20, second part, *Pleni sunt coeli.*

THE TWO-VOICE FUGUE

Two-voice fugues are extremely rare. There is only one among the forty-eight fugues contained in *The Well Tempered Clavier.* The beginning of it is illustrated in Example 2.

EX. 2   BACH - W.T.C., Vol. I, Fugue 10

Bach may well have felt that a third voice would have been too difficult to manage here, the subject and counter-subject being as swift and animated as they are. Or it is possible that he simply wished to include one two-voice fugue in the set and took advantage of the absence of other voices to use especially lively material. As can be seen here, the key plan in the exposition of a two-voice fugue is I V. This is unlike that of a two-part invention, in which the imitation is usually at the octave. After the exposition, the two-voice fugue proceeds in the same fashion as those that

* Here, as elsewhere in this book, the volume numbers cited in connection with Bach's organ works are those of the Peters Edition.

involve more voices, except, of course, that both voices must be present most of the time if a contrapuntal effect is to be maintained.

THE DOUBLE FUGUE

In a double fugue there are two subjects which appear *together* at some point in the work, not necessarily at the start. If a fugue makes use of two subjects which are treated one at a time but never combined, it is not considered a double fugue, but merely a fugue with two subjects.

There are three general possibilities for the construction of double fugues:

Type 1: Both subjects are announced together at the beginning. This is not to say that they will necessarily start at exactly the same time. In fact they seldom do, and the effect is better if they do not. In Example 3, for instance, a full measure of Subject I is heard before Subject II enters. Only the first two pairs of announcements are included in this example. As before, the singers' words have been omitted.

EX. 3   MOZART - Requiem (Kyrie from First Section)

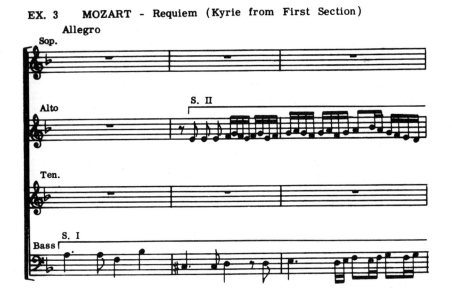

The Fugue (Concluded)

The two coordinate subjects are most likely to occur in adjacent voices, though in Example 3 they appear in parallel voices. Parallel voices are soprano and tenor, alto and bass. The usual treatment of the two subjects in the exposition follows the same general plan that applies to ordinary fugues; each subject is heard in each one of the voices in turn. After the exposition, there is no set plan. For the most part, the subjects, when they occur, appear together in order to bear out the double-fugue feeling. However, either one may occasionally be heard alone, or form the basis for development.

Examples

Bach, Organ Compositions, Vol. III, No. 9; Vol. IV, Nos. 8 and 10; Vol. V, No. 23.

Type 2: In this type of double fugue, Subject I first has its own exposition. After that, Subject II may be introduced

a) along with Subject I.

Example *

Bach, *The Art of Fugue,* No. 9 (Subject II enters in measure 35 in the soprano).

b) in an exposition of its own, during which Subject I does not appear. In this case, the two subjects are combined later on.

Examples

Bach, *The Well Tempered Clavier,* Vol. II, Fugue 18 (Subject II appears in measures 61–96, and is combined with Subject I from measure 97 to the end); Vol. II, Fugue 4 (Subject II is first heard in measure 20; it is combined with Subject I only intermittently through measure 47, but consistently from there to the end).

Type 3: Finally, there is a third kind of double fugue which might be described as a transitional form between the ordinary fugue and the more characteristic types of the double fugue mentioned under Types 1 and 2. In this kind of double fugue Subject II is introduced as counter-subject to the answer. In other words, the counter-subject is so distinctive and important, and recurs so consistently in the course of the fugue, that it ceases to play a secondary role and assumes a status equal to that of Subject I. Therefore, it is more accurately called a second subject. The first three announcements of a fugue of this type are shown in Example 4.

EX. 4   HANDEL - The Messiah "And with His Stripes Are We Healed"

* An interesting example of this form in contemporary music is the double fugue from Stravinsky's *Symphony of Psalms.*

191

Notice the startling similarity between the first subject here and the first subject in Example 3.

The difference between a counter-subject and an actual second subject in this type of double fugue is chiefly one of degree, since a good counter-subject also has distinctive qualities and reappears from time to time. Consequently, with certain fugues there might well be a difference of opinion as to whether the label "double fugue" is appropriate or not.   However, this does not destroy the validity of the category, into which some fugues very clearly fall.   In such fugues the exposition is sometimes extended beyond the usual proportions by an additional statement of the second subject, in order that the latter will be heard as many times as the first subject.

THE TRIPLE FUGUE

When a fugue has three subjects, the possibilities for presenting them, singly and in combination, are so numerous that it is impractical to attempt a complete listing.   Some of these possibilities can nevertheless be mentioned:

Type 1: Subject I enters alone and has a complete exposition.   After that Subjects II and III may

a) each be treated similarly in turn;

b) enter more or less together while Subject I drops out temporarily;

c) appear one at a time against Subject I (this is perhaps the most usual arrangement).

In any case, all three subjects will eventually be combined, such combination being the earmark of the real triple fugue.   The presence of three subjects is not in itself sufficient reason for calling a fugue "triple," according to accepted terminology.   For example, the "St. Anne" Fugue of Bach has three subjects, yet only two of these are combined.   Consequently, the work is probably most accurately described as a double fugue which makes use of three subjects.

Examples

Bach, *The Well Tempered Clavier*, Vol. I, Fugue 4 (Subject I to measure 35; Subject II then begins against Subject I; in measure 49 Subject III joins the first two; about 22 measures from the end, Subject II is abandoned while the other two continue in stretto fashion).

Bach, *The Art of Fugue*, Fugue 8 (Subject II enters in measure 39 against Subject I; in measure 94 Subject III, the one used in various guises throughout the volume, appears, and the other two drop out temporarily; I and II return together at measure 113; finally all three are combined for the first time at measure 147).

Type 2: In another species of triple fugue, Subjects I and II are announced together, and Subject III then joins them.

Examples

Beethoven, Symphony No. 3, second movement (*Adagio assai*), measures 114–133.   Subject III, in sixteenth notes, begins in measure 117, in the same voice that has just announced another subject in quarter notes and eighth notes.

The latter subject could be labeled either Subject I or Subject II, inasmuch as the first two subjects begin together.

Bach, Organ Compositions, Vol. I, finale of the Passacaglia (C minor).

Theoretically, there could be a type of triple fugue in which all three subjects are announced more or less together at the start. However, since this type is virtually unknown in musical literature, it will not be considered as a practical possibility here.

Whatever the particular arrangement used, the following general principles apply in the writing of triple fugues:

1) Each subject must be a strong line, with characteristic melodic and rhythmic features.

2) The three subjects must contrast with each other sufficiently to give an impression of independence. Possibly the most frequent and effective way of achieving this is to have them move in different values—for example, one chiefly in half notes, another in quarters, and the third in eighths.

3) Each subject must reappear frequently enough so that the ear will hear it as a major element in the composition, not simply as a secondary counterpoint. Here, as in certain kinds of double fugues, there could be a difference of opinion as to whether a particular melodic element should be considered an actual subject, or merely a counter-subject that recurs rather consistently. For example, Goetschius analyzes the fugue quoted in Example 10, Chapter 11, page 143, as one species of triple fugue. The author feels that it is more accurately classified as an ordinary three-voice fugue with counter-subjects that reappear with unusual regularity.

4) If all the possibilities for inversion of the voices are to be realized, each subject must work equally well as top, middle or bottom voice. However, it is unlikely that all these possibilities would be involved in any one fugue. In actual practice, therefore, this condition is usually not nearly as inclusive as it is in the general form given here.

Whereas inversion of the voices at the octave or multiples of it can generally be worked out without too much difficulty, inversion at other intervals is likely to prove extremely difficult in triple counterpoint, and is seldom seen.

FUGUES WITH MORE THAN THREE SUBJECTS

Except for the famous quintuple fugue in the last movement of Mozart's C major ("Jupiter") Symphony, fugues involving more than three actual subjects are almost unknown in musical literature. The excerpt from the Mozart movement quoted in Chapter 11, page 144, as an example of invertible counterpoint showed the five subjects combined.

THE FUGHETTA AND THE FUGATO

A *fughetta* is simply a small fugue. Abundant examples can be seen in Bach's organ works, Volumes V and VI in particular.

A *fugato* is a passage treated in fugal style, that is, with imitative entrances as in a fugue exposition. Unlike the fughetta, it is not usually a separate piece of music, but is generally a section of a longer work.

THE CONCERT FUGUE

A concert fugue is one in which there is particular emphasis on brilliance and dramatic effect. Freedom of treatment is also characteristic, and is likely to take these forms:

1) The number of voices may be increased at times, and chords may be added, so that the texture becomes more homophonic than contrapuntal.

2) The episodes may be considerably freer and more extended.

3) The form of the whole may be more sectional than usual, with decided cadences and strong contrasts between sections.

4) The subject itself may be more colorful, more animated, or longer than usual.

Concert fugues are often part of a larger work, such as a set of variations or an opera; sometimes they are preceded by an introductory movement. But they seldom stand alone as separate works.

Examples

Bach, *Chromatic Fantasy and Fugue* (for clavier).
Brahms-Handel, *Variations* for piano, the *Finale.*
Franck, *Prelude, Chorale and Fugue.*
Weinberger, *Polka and Fugue* from *Schwanda, der Dudelsackpfeifer.*

THE FUGUE FANTASIA

In a fugue fantasia, or fantasia fugue, the material is treated with great freedom, especially after the exposition, which is usually strict. Sometimes a small portion of the subject forms the basis for extended elaboration or fanciful development in later portions of the work.

Example

Bach, *The Well Tempered Clavier*, Vol. II, Fugue 3.

The Fugue (Concluded)

COMBINATIONS OF CHORALE AND FUGUE

The chorale and fugue may be combined in various ways:

Type 1: There is a fugal exposition, toward the end of which the first line of a chorale appears against the fugal texture, in a voice that has rested until then. The fugue proceeds, and successive lines of the chorale are superimposed on it from time to time. As a rule, the fugue subject is freely derived from the first, or another, portion of the chorale melody.

Examples
Bach, Organ Compositions, Vol. VI, No. 30; Vol. VII, Nos. 39a and 39b.

Type 2: This type, known variously as "motet fugue," "chorale motet," and "chorale fugue," is like Type 1 except that each line of the chorale is introduced by a fugal exposition based on a subject derived from the line that is about to be heard. That is, instead of having one subject for the entire fugue, we have as many subjects as there are lines (phrases) in the chorale.

Examples
Bach, Organ Compositions, Vol. VI, Nos. 21, 28; Vol. VII, Nos. 50, 55, 58.
Bach, Cantatas Nos. 16, 27, 58, 60, 73, 95, the first movement in each case.

Type 3: In certain fugues the subject or subjects derive from a chorale melody as in Types 1 and 2, but the chorale melody itself is not stated.

Examples
Bach, Organ Compositions, Vol. VI, Nos. 11, 20, 33; Vol. VII, No. 60.

Even though all three of these types involve fugal treatment, they are usually thought of as chorale forms rather than fugue forms. Discussion of them was reserved for this chapter only because fugue had not been studied at the time the chorale forms were taken up.

THE GROUP FUGUE

This name, though not in general use, has been adopted here to describe fugues which use the same sectional technique as Type 2, above, but without involving chorale material. In other words, such fugues consist of a series of fughettas, each based on a different subject. This is actually the plan of the early *ricercare,* as it existed before composers began to tie the various sections together by the use of a common subject.

Bach, Organ Compositions, Vol. III, No. 6 (three sections, the third using the same subject as the first).

Bach, B minor Mass, No. 19, last division *(Vivace e allegro), Et Expecto* and *Amen* (four subjects).

FUGUE WRITING AS AFFECTED BY THE MEDIUM

In a fugue, as in any other type of composition, the character of the music is almost certain to be influenced to some degree by the medium for which it is written.

When a fugue is designed for performance on the piano, the spacings and movements of the voices must obviously be kept within the technical limitations of the two hands, and of course the color and dynamic potentialities of the instrument in its various registers should be kept in mind.

In writing for the organ, we have several added possibilities. A voice may be played on the pedals, as long as it is not too fast or intricate. The instrument has a tremendous dynamic range, and we can apply different dynamics to the various voices if they are on different manuals. Also, the stops provide a wealth of different colors, and notes may be sustained as long as desired.

In fugues for the string quartet or other chamber groups, we are free to indulge in wide spacings, frequent crossing of voices, and melodic patterns idiomatic to the instruments involved.

The writing of vocal fugues must obviously be approached with an eye to the ranges of the various voices, the color and relative power of each register within these ranges, and the question of what is vocally practical and effective. The subjects of such fugues are likely to be more lyrical and sustained than those of instrumental fugues. It must be remembered that most of the examples in this book are taken from instrumental literature, and that as a result they do not, as a whole, serve as good models for vocal writing. Consequently, the student who elects to write fugues or other contrapuntal forms for choral groups would do well to examine as much contrapuntal choral music as possible before attempting such writing.

Because the orchestra offers tremendous possibilities in color, dynamic range, and technical versatility, fugues written for it may be of almost any character, and it involves no limitations as to the number of voices or their movement. Orchestral fugues tend to be big in conception, and to exploit at times the effective device of making lines stand out sharply from each other by allotting different orchestral colors to them.

The Fugue (Concluded)

It is possible, of course, to write music simply as music, without any particular performing idiom in mind. Bach's *The Art of Fugue*, which has been mentioned many times in this book, is such a work. Fortunately, it is performable on various instruments such as the string quartet, the organ, and the piano, so that it can be appreciated in terms of actual sound, and not merely on paper.

SUGGESTED ASSIGNMENTS

1. *Analyze the following and be prepared to present an oral analysis in class:*
   a) *Either Fugue 4 or Fugue 22 in Volume I of* The Well Tempered Clavier *(both five-voice fugues)*
   b) *Fugue 10 in Volume I (two-voice fugue)*
   c) *One example of each type of double fugue*
   d) *One example of each type of triple fugue*
   e) *One example of each type of chorale fugue*
   f) *One example of the "group fugue"*
   g) *One example of the concert fugue*
   h) *Fugues from Bach's* The Art of Fugue *as specified by the instructor.*
2. *Write the following:*
   a) *The exposition of a double fugue, Type 1*
   b) *A complete double fugue, any type*
   c) *The exposition of a triple fugue, either type*
   d) *A complete triple fugue, either type*
   e) *A chorale fugue, any type, or a group fugue*
   f) *A concert fugue*

Bibliography

Apel, Willi, *Harvard Dictionary of Music.* Cambridge: Harvard U. P., Cambridge, 1950.

AtKisson, Harold F., *Basic Counterpoint.* New York: McGraw, 1956.

Bairstow, Sir Edward Cuthbert, *Counterpoint and Harmony.* London: Macmillan, 1945.

Cherubini, Luigi, *A Treatise on Counterpoint and Fugue,* translated by Mary C. Clarke, revised by Joseph Bennett. London: Novello.

Dickinson, A. E. F., *The Art of J. S. Bach.* London: Duckworth, 1936, revised 1950.

————, *Bach's Fugal Works.* New York: Pitman, 1956.

DuBois, Théodore, *Traité de Contrepoint et de Fugue.* Paris: Heugel, 1901.

Erickson, Robert, *The Structure of Music.* New York: Noonday Press, 1955.

Fuller-Maitland, J. A., *The "48," Bach's Wohltemperirtes Klavier.* London: Oxford U. P., 1925.

Fux, Johann Joseph, *Steps to Parnassus,* translated and edited by Alfred Mann and John St. Edmunds. New York: Norton, 1945.

Gedalge, André, *Traité de la Fugue.* Paris: Enoch, 1890.

Goetschius, Percy, *Applied Counterpoint.* New York: G. Schirmer, fifth edition, 1915.

————, *Exercises in Elementary Counterpoint.* New York: G. Schirmer, 1910.

Gray, Cecil, *The Forty-eight Preludes and Fugues of J. S. Bach.* London: Oxford U. P., 1938.

Jadassohn, Salamon, *A Course of Instruction in Canon and Fugue,* translated by Gustav Wolff, Leipzig: Breitkopf and Härtel, 1929.

Kanitz, Ernest, *A Counterpoint Workbook.* Ann Arbor, Mich.: Edwards Bros., 1947.

Kitson, C. H., *The Art of Counterpoint.* London: Oxford U. P., 1907.

————, *Invertible Counterpoint and Canon.* London: Oxford U. P., 1927.

————, *Studies in Fugue.* London: Oxford U. P., 1928.

————, *The Elements of Fugal Construction.* London: Oxford U. P., 1929.

————, *Applied Strict Counterpoint.* Oxford: Clarendon Press, 1931.

————, *Counterpoint for Beginners.* London: Oxford U. P., 1937.

Bibliography

Levarie, Siegmund, *Fugue and Form*. Copyright by Siegmund Levarie, 1941 (paper presented before the convention of the American Musicological Society, mid-West Chapter).

Lytle, Victor Vaughn, *The Theory and Practice of Strict Counterpoint*. Philadelphia: Ditson, 1940.

MacPherson, Stewart, *Studies in the Art of Counterpoint*. London: Joseph Williams, 1927.

McHose, Allen Irvine, *The Contrapuntal Harmonic Technique of the 18th Century*. New York: Appleton, 1947.

Morris, R. O., *Foundations of Practical Harmony and Counterpoint*. London: Macmillan, 1936.

————, *Introduction to Counterpoint*. London: Oxford U. P., 1953.

Oldroyd, George, *The Technique and Spirit of Fugue*. London: Oxford U. P., 1948.

————, *Polyphonic Writing for Voices in Six or Eight Parts*. London: Oxford U. P., 1953.

Orem, Preston Ware, *Manual of Fugue*. Bryn Mawr, Pa.: Presser, 1939.

Pearce, Charles W., *Students' Counterpoint*. New York: G. Schirmer, 1926.

Piston, Walter, *Counterpoint*. New York: Norton, 1947.

Porter, Quincy, *A Study of Fugue Writing*. Boston: Loomis, 1951.

Procter, Leland H., *Tonal Counterpoint*. Dubuque, Iowa: Brown, 1957.

Prout, Ebenezer, *Fugue*. London: Augener, 1891.

————, *Double Counterpoint and Canon*. London: Augener, 1891.

————, *Fugal Analysis*. London: Augener, 1892.

Richardson, A. Madeley, *Helps to Fugue Writing*. New York: H. W. Gray, 1930.

————, *Fundamental Counterpoint*. New York: Am. B. Co., 1936.

200

Index

202

Eternal canons, 111
Exposition:
  cadence in, 157
  defined, 154
  four-voice fugue, 157–61
  in general plan of fugue, 147
  special devices in, 164–65
  three-voice fugue, 154–57
  second (counter), 165

F

False entries, 181
Fantasia fugue, 195
Fantasias, chorale, 122, 133
Fermata, 123
Fifth Mass (Haydn), 148
Figurated harmony, 86
First species counterpoint, 28–30
Five-voice fugue, 186–87
Fixed counterpoint, 61
Follower, defined, 99
Foundations of Practical Harmony and Counterpoint (Morris), 3
Fourth species counterpoint, 50–57
Four-Voice Canon (Albrechtsberger), 104
Four-voice canons, 103, 104
Four-voice fugue exposition, 157–61
Franck:
  music of, 80
  Prelude, Chorale and Fugue, 195
  Sonata for Violin and Piano, 115–16
  Symphony in D. minor, 5
Frederick the Great, 114
Free counterpoint, 2, 86
Free material, 61, 64
Free voice, 115, 156
French Suite No. 1 (Bach), 38, 41
French Suite No. 2 (Bach), 21
French Suite No. 5 (Bach), 4
Frescobaldi, *Fugue*, 148
Fugato, defined, 195
Fughetta:
  Bach, 122
  chorale, 133–34
  defined, 195
Fugue:
  added 3rds in, 175
  analysis of, 176–82
  answer in, 149–54 (*see also* Answer)
  bipartite, 184–85
  chorale, 133–34
  coda in, 167, 175–76
  combined with chorale, 196

Fugue (*Cont.*)
  concert, 195
  counter-exposition in, 165
  counter-subject of, 155–56, 159–60
  described, 146–47
  devices applied in middle entries, 171–73
  double, 189–93
  episodes in, 167–70 (*see also* Episodes)
  exposition of:
    defined, 154
    four-voice, 157–61
    special devices in, 164–65
    three-voice, 154–57
  fantasia, 195
  final portion of, 173–76
  five-voice, 186–87
  for chamber group, 197
  free voice in, 156
  group, 196–97
  middle entries in, 170–73 (*see also* Middle entries)
  with more than three subjects, 194
  with no counter-subject, 160
  order of keys in, 156, 158–59
  orchestral, 197
  pedal point in, 173, 174–75
  plan of four-voice exposition, 161
  plan of three-voice exposition, 157
  procedure after exposition, 167
  recapitulation in, 173–74
  scholastic, 182–83
  sectional, 185
  six or more voices, 187–88
  stretto, 163–64
  "strophic form," 185
  subject of, 147–49 (*see also* Subject)
    as related to answer, 163–64
    relation to material following, 161–63
  tonal imitation in, 150–53
  triple, 193–94
  two-voice, 188–89
  vocal, 197
  writing, as affected by medium, 197–98
Fugue and Form (Levarie), 184, 184n, 185
Fugue (Frescobaldi), 148
Fugue in C Major (Buxtehude), 44
Fugue in C Minor (Bach), 95
Fugue in D Minor (Bach), for organ, 152
Fugue in E Minor (Bach), for organ, 148
Fugue in G Minor (Bach), for organ, 148, 153

205

G

Gedalge, André, 182, 183
Gegenfuge, 164
Goldberg Variations (Bach), 102
   third, 101
   twenty-seventh, 102
Gradus ad Parnassum (Fux), 1
Group fugues, 196–97

H

Handel:
   Concerto Grosso in C, 94
   Messiah, The, 7
      "And with His Stripes Are We
       Healed," 191–92
Harmonic intervals, 100, 102, 103
Harmonic rhythm, 8
Harmony:
   as background of melody, 7–9, 10
   change of, 132
   chorale prelude and, 123
   chromaticism and, 38–43
   counterpoint and, 3
   figurated, 86
   implied in counterpoint, 22–24
   in three-voice counterpoint, 76
   tonic, 9
Haydn:
   Andante con Variazioni, 51
   as counterpoint student, 1
   Fifth Mass, 148
   Sonata, 34
   Symphony No. 2 ("London"), 137
Herzlich thut mich verlangen (Bach), 124

I

Imitation, tonal, 91–95, 150–54 (*see also*
   Tonal imitation)
In Dulci Jubilo (Bach), chorale prelude
   for organ, 117
Infinite canons, 111
Intermediate tones, 88
Intervals:
   canons at, 101
   changes in, 62, 70
   classified, 20–22
   essential, 19
   harmonic, in canonic writing, 100, 102,
      103
   inversion (*see* Inversion)
   in second species counterpoint, 34–35

Intervals (*Cont.*)
   table of inversion, 142
   time, in canonic writing, 99–100, 104
   unessential, 19
   vertical, 29–30
Inventionen, 60 (*see also* Inventions)
Inventions (*see also* Bach Inventions)
   analysis of, 63–72
      terms and symbols, 64
      three-part, 96–98
   augmentation in, 63
   changes in interval in, 70
   construction and content, 61–62
   defined, 61
   development of, 62–63
   examples of, 64–70 (*see also* Bach In-
      ventions)
   second motive in, 68
   three-part, 87–98 (*see also* Three-part
      inventions)
   two-part, defined, 61
Inversion, 135–45
   accidentals and, 141
   contrary motion (*see* Contrary motion)
   defined, 135
   at intervals other than the octave, 138–
      41
   intervals, *table,* 142
   at the octave, 135–38
   possibilities of, 139–40
   of subject and counter-subject, 155
   of three or more voices, 143–44
   of voices in triple fugue, 194
Invertible counterpoint, 44–45, 135–45
      (*see also* Inversion)
   artificial and natural, 138
   double, 135
   inversion and, 63
   inversion at intervals other than the
      octave, 138–41
   inversion at the octave, 135–38
   quadruple, 144
   triple, 143
   writing, 141–43

K

Kennan, *Canon in Inversion at 4th Below,*
   120
Keys:
   Bach's use of in inventions, 61, 62
   dominant, 61, 62, 65, 87, 156, 158, 159
   episodes and, 167–170
   motive in different, 61–62
   order of, in fugues, 156, 158–59

207

209

210

211